BABY SIGN LANGUAGE

by Diane Ryan

Publisher: Mike Sanders
Editor: Christopher Stolle
Cover Designer: Rebecca Batchelor
Illustrator: Hannah Sun
Layout: Ayanna Lacey
Technical Editor: Lora Heller
Proofreader: Amy J. Schneider
Indexer: Celia McCoy

First American Edition, 2021
Published in the United States by DK Publishing
6081 E. 82nd Street, Indianapolis, IN 46250

Library of Congress Catalog Number: 2020950792
ISBN 978-1-61564-994-5

DK books are available at special discounts when purchased
in bulk for sales promotions, premiums, fund-raising, or
educational use. For details, contact: DK Publishing Special
Markets, 1450 Broadway, Suite 801, New York, NY 10018
SpecialSales@dk.com

Printed and bound in the United States of America

Reprinted and updated from
The Complete Idiot's Guide® to Baby Sign Language, Second Edition

For the curious
www.dk.com

Contents

Part 1 Baby Sign Language Basics 1

1 What Is Baby Sign Language?.........................3

A Simple and Natural Way to Communicate 4

Why Teach Sign Language to a
Hearing Baby? 4

The Biggest Misconception............................. 5

What Will Your Baby Be Able to Tell You?......... 5

How Is This Possible? 6

Can All Babies Do This? 6

Is This Appropriate for Deaf Babies? 7

Back to the Beginning.................................... 7

Doctors in the House 8

2 How Your Baby (and You) Will Benefit 11

More Research Findings................................ 12

How Exactly Will Your Baby Benefit? 13

What's In It for Parents? 15

Bragging About Your Bilingual Baby 15

3 Why and How It Works 17

Making Connections 18

Brain Development....................................... 18

How to Best Boost Your Baby's IQ.................. 18

The Sign Language Connection 18

It's All in the Timing.................................... 19

When to Introduce Signs 19

When to Expect Results 22

Part 2 Ready, Set, Sign! 25

4 Introducing Baby's First Signs...................... 27

Traditional Method vs. Express Method........... 28

Sign Language Categories............................. 28

The First Three Signs: MORE, EAT, and
MILK 28

The Sign for MORE 29

The Sign for EAT 30

The Sign for MILK 31

Teaching Other Important Signs 32

The Sign for HURT/PAIN............................. 32

The Sign for HELP..................................... 33

The Sign for DIAPER CHANGE................... 34

Looking for Signs of Progress....................... 35

Recognizing Early Attempts.......................... 35

Ten Signing Suggestions.............................. 36

5 The Express Version 37

How Soon Can You Expect Results?............... 38

What's the Big Deal About 11 Months? 38

Why the Big Rush?...................................... 38

Step-by-Step Express Method 38

Week 1: Introducing the First Sign.................. 40

Week 2: Staying Focused and On Track 40

Introducing Additional Signs.......................... 42

Deciding Where to Go From Here 43

An Important Note for Parents-in-Waiting 43

**6 Increasing Your Baby's Sign Language
Vocabulary 45**

The Sign for DON'T TOUCH........................ 46

The Sign for GENTLE TOUCH..................... 47

Where to Go From Here 47

Introducing Additional Signs.......................... 48

Combining Signs 51

Signing in Sentences................................... 51

Your Little Conversationalist 51

Some Helpful Reminders 52

7 Staying the Course 53

Staying Motivated....................................... 54

Motivational Tips and Tactics 54

Finding the Time.. 55

Request Help 56
Reinforcements 57

Part 3 The Advanced Signer 59

8 Sign Language for Toddlers............... 61
Why It's a Good Idea.................. 62
Information Overload....................... 62
Top 10 Reasons to Sign With a Toddler 62
Your Job as Translator..................... 63
Some Advice Before Getting Started 63
Your Plan of Action...................... 63
What About Talking?....................... 64

9 Learning by Example................... 65
Teaching Categories 66
Food and Drink Signs....................... 66
Good Manners Signs 69
Behavior and Safety Signs.................... 71
Activities and Games Signs.................... 74
Feelings and Emotions Signs.................... 76
Animal Signs 77

10 Potty Training and Sign Language................... 79
How Sign Language Helps With
Potty Training................. 80
Getting an Earlier Start..................... 80
It's About Being Ready.................. 81
Beginning the Process 81
Tips and Techniques 84
The Reward System..................... 85

11 Look Who Can Talk!..................... 87
Keep on Signing 88
Why They'll Speak Rather Than Sign............. 88
How It Will All Play Out................... 88
Taking Corrective Action 89
You and Your Baby's Secret Signs.................... 90

Dealing with Speech and Language
Development Concerns............................. 92
Sign Language and Children With
Special Needs......................... 95

Appendixes

A Baby Sign Language Dictionary...................... 97

B Getting Everyone Involved............................ 175

C Frequently Asked Questions About
Baby Sign Language 177

D Activities and Games to Encourage
Your Baby to Sign 181

E Resources................................. 185

F Baby Sign Language Journal 189

Index 197

Part 1

Baby Sign Language Basics

Imagine communicating with your baby before they can speak. This is what baby sign language is all about. In this section, you'll learn why you might teach sign language to a hearing child as well as how sign language can help with speech development.

Chapter 1

What Is Baby Sign Language?

Baby sign language is a way to communicate with your baby before they can speak by teaching them basic helpful signs. It's a way to bridge the gap between nonverbal stages and the time when they can actually talk. In fact, you can continue to teach your child sign language well beyond that stage.

You have a number of options available when it comes to signing. One has to do with why you want to do it in the first place. If you're like most hearing parents, you're considering it as an interim method of communication before your baby's first words. Other parents think of it as a way to begin a lifelong skill. There's one thing everyone can agree on: To be successful, learning sign language has to be fun for everyone involved.

Baby sign language isn't part of the craze to create smarter, higher-thinking infants and children. And while you might find baby sign language books and DVDs in the same aisle as the so-called IQ boosters, they're not similar. Research shows that without consistent engagement, all the mental stimulation programs don't do much more than entertain a baby. To boost a baby's mental acuity, human interaction needs to be part of the learning environment. And human interaction is what signing with your baby is all about.

There are some differences of opinion as to how much of an IQ boost sign language really creates. Some say not much at all; some research has found as much as a 20-point gain. But even if you totally discount a higher IQ as a signing advantage, numerous benefits to sign language can lead to immediate and long-term value.

Parents feel good about teaching a baby to sign because it's natural. It's based on an instinctive tendency to gesture. It also enhances communication, builds stronger connections in families, and reduces a pre-verbal baby's frustration when they can't get their point across. It will help you develop a closer relationship with your little one and form a tighter bond. Plus, your baby will really love the experience! If there are cerebral fringe benefits beyond that—and most scientists tell us there are—then all the better.

A Simple and Natural Way to Communicate

Teaching a baby to sign is simple. Yes, signing with your baby does involve patience and dedication, but the benefits are well worth your time investment.

When you teach your baby to sign, you'll use signs that are part of American Sign Language (ASL), the official language of the Deaf community in the United States. While your baby will approximate or adapt some signs that challenge their emerging motor skills, parents are encouraged to model ASL. Many parents consider this the first step in introducing a second language to their child. Although you'll be using authentic ASL signs, you *don't* have to learn an entire sign language. You'll start with a few basic signs and then you can add as many as you like from there.

Depending on your baby's age, they might already *be* signing! Babies raise their hands to be picked up. They point to things they want. And think how easy it is to teach a baby to wave "bye-bye." That means that as you teach your baby to sign, you're also supporting and empowering what already comes naturally.

This is a fantastic way to develop a closer connection with your child. It's a great opportunity to find out what your baby's thinking. It's a way to look into their world through *their* eyes—a window into their thoughts. Why just guess what your baby wants or needs? If you teach them to sign, they can tell you themselves.

Why Teach Sign Language to a Hearing Baby?

It used to be that sign language was associated only with Deaf culture. The benefits of teaching sign language to hearing children weren't widely recognized. After all, what was the purpose? They would speak eventually because they could hear speech all around them. But then along came someone who tested that idea.

While working as an interpreter for the Deaf in Alaska in the late 1970s, Joseph Garcia noticed that the hearing babies of Deaf parents communicated at a much earlier age than children of hearing parents. That observation piqued his interest, sparked additional research, and resulted in a practical system to teach the technique to parents. You'll learn more about Joseph Garcia and his "Sign With Your Baby" program later in this chapter. But for now, credit him with replacing the question of "Why?" with "Why not?"

Some might say: "I already know what my baby wants and needs. I can tell by the way they cry. Their hunger cry is different from their cry for attention. And when they're in pain, I can tell that too." While there's some truth to this, a *signing* baby can share more *specific* information about what they want or need, plus they'll gain a lot of secondary benefits along the way.

In fact, babies who sign are less frustrated, have closer bonds with their parents and caregivers, develop larger vocabularies, become better readers, and "outsmart" babies who don't sign.

The Biggest Misconception

Is there a downside to teaching your baby sign language? If you teach your baby to sign, will that delay their speech? Actually, if you teach your baby a few simple signs, they'll speak *earlier*. Now you can add "earlier speech" to the list of benefits. It's logical to think that teaching your baby to sign might be giving them a reason not to talk. But when you introduce a specific sign to your baby, you'll *talk* with them at the same time. Always *say* the word as you make the sign. For a hearing child to best develop speech and language, it's essential to speak as you sign.

Research tells us that parents of signing babies spend more time with them. Suddenly, the baby stage takes on a new dimension. It becomes less custodial. Signing babies can actually *participate* in the family dynamic. The family spends more time together playing, reading, labeling things, asking questions, responding to those same questions, and talking while also making language visual.

What Will Your Baby Be Able to Tell You?

Consider this scenario: It's 2:30 a.m. and your 12-month-old starts to cry. You get up and go to their room. You run through the mental checklist. You feel their diaper. Totally dry. You offer them some water. They cry even louder. You put your lips to the baby's forehead. No fever. Now they're screaming.

You put the tips of your two index fingers together in their sight line. It's the sign for PAIN. They make the same sign in front of their mouth. You realize they're teething again. You get their medicine and rub it on their gums. A few minutes later, they stop crying and fall back asleep. And you go back to bed.

Pretty amazing, don't you think? You now have a baby who can sign and can tell you when they're in pain and also *where it hurts*. They can tell you when they're hungry or thirsty or if they need help. They can even tell you when they need a diaper change! Truly extraordinary, especially when you consider a baby can "tell" you all these things before they're able to utter a single word.

How Is This Possible?

Research has shown that while babies lack the oral motor skills to speak, they do have the ability to understand and use language as early as four to six months—if they're given the right tools and guidance. While speech might be more than six months away, a baby's receptive language skills significantly improve after only six months on the planet. So does their ability to manipulate objects with their hands. No need to wait for your baby to speak their first words. They're ready to communicate *now*.

Speaking of *speaking*, think about how really complicated the act of talking is, especially to a baby. For adults, it's second nature. They have something to say and out it comes. But speech is an intricate and exacting dance. Depending on the sounds or words you want to say, your tongue must be in a precise location, your lips need to coordinate with your teeth, and you have to control your breathing to direct the flow of air—all the while making sure you have enough left over so you don't pass out. A baby's brain needs about a year or more to even begin to take on that task.

But that's just on the mechanical side. Before your baby says their first word, they need to hear that word many times and have some idea of its meaning. They have to be able to differentiate between sounds and words as well as recognize where words begin and end. To a baby, a family discussion sounds like a constant stream of gibberish. But somehow—miraculously—and in such a very short period of time, a baby will sort it all out and be able to speak. How can you help them simplify and accelerate the process toward speech? By teaching them a few basic signs.

Can All Babies Do This?

Gesturing is a natural tendency for a baby. It's something they'll do even if you don't introduce sign language. Babies are mimics. They take their lead from the people who surround them. They learn to speak by listening to you. And they'll learn to sign by watching you. Their natural gestures will become meaningful, language-based signs.

Whether a baby will sign has little to do with the baby. Of course, their individual personalities come into play, but all babies can learn to sign. How fast they'll learn and how many signs they'll make are the things in question. But you already know the variable, right? The degree of signing success a baby achieves is in direct proportion to the level of dedication and enthusiasm of their parents.

Is This Appropriate for Deaf Babies?

Some parents have long-range intentions when they start teaching their baby sign language. But most parents will only sign until their baby's speech surpasses their signing ability. Obviously, a Deaf baby has a much greater challenge than a hearing child. They need a lifelong skill to be able to communicate. Whether a Deaf baby's taught lip reading or sign language or a combination of both, they need a more structured program specifically designed for that tiny individual and their particular level of hearing loss. Because most Deaf babies are born to hearing parents, this accessible language is essential in their environment. Babies born to Deaf signing parents will naturally learn sign as their native language.

The techniques presented in this book are designed to enhance a baby's ability to communicate, not establish it. These demonstrations are based on the premise that the baby has the ability to hear and will eventually produce the sounds and words that are being presented to them. Will teaching these signs to a Deaf baby hurt them? Of course not. But this program doesn't go far enough nor is it comprehensive enough to address a Deaf baby's special needs. But if you're a hearing parent of a Deaf baby, this book can be an important resource as you connect with your local Deaf community.

Back to the Beginning

You might still be somewhat skeptical or simply inquisitive about the origins of baby sign language. You need more information, especially when your baby's involved. Who are these people who came up with this idea? What are their credentials?

The interest in teaching sign language to hearing babies began in the late 1980s with two separate and significant research projects conducted by Joseph Garcia, a student at Alaska Pacific University, and the team of Linda Acredolo and Susan Goodwyn, then PhDs at the University of California at Davis. While their research was independent and distinct, they had one thing in common: They used what they had around the house to formulate and test their theories: their kids.

As an undergraduate student, Joseph became fascinated with the idea of communicating through gestures or signs. While no one was Deaf in his family, he thought learning sign language would be interesting and he began to study it in earnest. Once he had a solid grasp of ASL, Joseph was certified as an interpreter for the Deaf and became involved—personally and professionally—with the Deaf community. It resulted in an observation that changed his life—and the lives of many to come.

While spending time with Deaf friends, Joseph noticed that the hearing babies of Deaf parents were able to communicate basic wants and needs at around 10 months of age. How was that possible? Simple. They saw their parents signing and their parents signed directly to them.

Joseph contrasted this with the communicative ability of hearing babies with hearing parents. Around that age (10 months), they hardly communicated at all! Intrigued by this disparity, Joseph decided to make it the focus of his master's thesis.

During his research, Joseph discovered that hearing children were able to produce simple signs at around eight months and some exceptional children as early as six months. Certainly, this was far earlier than any baby could articulate any *spoken* word.

Joseph also found that once a signing child began to speak, they had a better grasp of grammar and language in general. Using his infant sons Stratton and Damien as "test subjects," Joseph validated his theories firsthand on the home front.

Joseph's program evolved into the popular book/video program *Sign With Your Baby: How to Communicate With Infants Before They Can Speak* (see Appendix E). Like this program, it's based on using ASL as the basis for communicating with a baby through signing. For more information, visit sign2me.com/sign2me_WP_Test-1.

Doctors in the House

The findings of the Acredolo–Goodwyn team also stemmed from simple observations of a child's behavior. In 1982, when her daughter Kate was a year old, psychology professor Linda Acredolo noticed she made an "itsy bitsy spider" with her hands whenever she saw one of the critters. When Kate spotted a flower, she would wiggle her nose as if sniffing it.

Then there was a third event—one that's especially interesting. It was time for Kate's 12-month checkup at the pediatrician's office. While they were in the waiting room, Kate was naturally attracted by the large aquarium there and toddled over for a better look. But then, according to Linda, she did something strange. She started to *blow*.

Dr. Mom was puzzled by the behavior. After the appointment, she took Kate home for a nap. As she put her down in her crib, Linda activated the mobile that hung over it. It was fashioned of brightly colored fish, and to make it rotate, Linda had to blow on it. Instantly, she became aware of the connection her daughter had made. Without any instruction, Kate was communicating with her own form of sign language.

As you might imagine, the learned professor wanted to find out more. She had lots of questions: Do all children do this or just my daughter? Are there other signs or gestures Kate might be using that I'm unaware of?

Linda partnered with her colleague, Susan Goodwyn, then professor of psychology and child development at California State University at Stanislaus and an associate researcher at the University of California. They studied, observed, and questioned other parents. As scientists, they did things the right way. Backed by a federal grant, they compared babies who signed with babies who didn't. Then they followed and documented their progress. We'll look into those findings in greater detail in Chapter 2.

Based on their research, *Baby Signs: How to Talk With Your Baby Before Your Baby Can Talk* (see Appendix E) was published. The program promotes a short-term sign language experience and recommends a combination of adapted "baby friendly" ASL as well as signs and gestures that parents and babies create on their own. For more information, visit www.babysignstoo.com.

Many baby sign language books and videos are available that are based on the findings of the baby sign language pioneers. No matter which program you use, remember that your goal is not just for your baby to sign but also to *speak*.

How Your Baby (and You) Will Benefit

Linda Acredolo and Susan Goodwyn knew they needed financial backing to continue their research. In 1989, they headed for the National Institutes of Health and managed to convince potential investors that studying the long-term effects of teaching hearing babies sign language was worthy of a grant. Their earlier research had convinced the dynamic duo of the short-term benefits. Now they needed to know more, especially the advantages (or disadvantages) of teaching sign language to hearing babies.

More than 140 families with 11-month-old babies were chosen for the study. Each family had to fit certain criteria to make sure all the babies were at a similar stage of development. Family income and education were considered as well as each baby's sex, birth order, and ability to vocalize.

One-third of the families were shown how to use sign language. Another third were encouraged to speak to their babies more often than they would normally. The remaining families were the control group. They were told to simply do what comes naturally—to continue caring for their babies as they would normally. None of the groups were aware of the other participants and no one had any idea what the whole thing was about.

Each family agreed to spend two years in the study. Their progress would be monitored, and after 24 months, the signing babies would be tested to see if there were any benefits or negative side effects. Then comparisons would be made with the other groups.

Keep in mind that the results mentioned in these studies are based on the "average" and will not be the same for each child. That means your baby might not reach these lofty heights—but they could also reach even higher.

Acredolo and Goodwyn found the following:

- At 24 months, the signing babies had the vocabularies of 27- or 28-month-olds.

- At 24 months, they used significantly longer sentences.

- At 36 months, the signers spoke like 47-month-olds—almost a full year ahead.

Bottom line? The signing babies outperformed all other groups. But scientists always want to know more. In this case, it was whether there'd be any long-term effects to teaching a hearing baby to sign. So they waited eight years and paid those same families another visit.

Now age eight, the children were tested to see what happened after all that time. The reviews were all positive. In general, when tested eight years later, the babies who had learned some basic sign language had better language and cognitive skills than those who hadn't. Signing babies also demonstrated an above-average understanding of English, and their grammar and syntax were more advanced.

More Research Findings

Dr. Marilyn Daniels, who was a professor of communication arts and sciences at Penn State University, is probably the most prolific researcher on children and sign language. While she acknowledged the Acredolo–Goodwyn studies, she decided to dig deeper into the correlation between sign language and intellectual and academic development.

Dr. Daniels's research stemmed from an observation her graduate students made. They wondered why the hearing children of Deaf parents seemed to do so well in reading and writing. Logical thinking told them that because these children lived in an environment without speech, they should be struggling in these areas, not excelling in them. So Dr. Daniels did what any self-respecting academician would do: She designed a study. In fact, numerous studies. The results of her research were first presented in 1994:

- Signing children have better recognition of letters and sounds than nonsigners. They're also better spellers and have larger vocabularies.

- Children who sign speak better and have more advanced communication skills than nonsigners.

- Children who had been taught American Sign Language had higher reading levels than those who had no ASL instruction.

Dr. Daniels's work was published in *Dancing With Words: Signing for Hearing Children's Literacy* (see Appendix E). In addition to encouraging parents to sign with babies and children, she recommended that teachers incorporate ASL into their curriculum. Educators who have followed her advice claim that not only do children enjoy the experience but that sign language also actually accelerates literacy and learning.

How Exactly Will Your Baby Benefit?

It bears repeating that the benefits mentioned in this section are based on the "average." Your baby might not do as well or they might outperform them all.

Emotional Benefits

There are countless gifts you can give your baby. But signing parents give theirs something you just can't can buy: emotional well-being. This includes developing the following:

- **Less frustration.** When you give your baby a way to express their feelings, you can begin to eliminate reasons for frustration. They'll discover that signing empowers them and that it's more productive than crying, whining, or throwing a fit. They now have the tools to communicate specific information to you.

- **Greater self-esteem and self-confidence.** Studies show that being understood by a grown-up is important for any child. A signing baby grows up thinking well of themselves because of the positive responses of those around them.

- **A closer parent-infant bond.** When you sign with your baby, you'll spend more time together—quality time with positive interactions. So much face-to-face time is even more valuable in this age of technology. You'll find parenting becomes custodial and reactive. And your baby will discover much sooner who's boss.

Once your baby has an effective way to communicate, they'll play a more active role in the family and develop a closer bond with siblings and caregivers. They'll be able to make demands and have their requests fulfilled. Signing babies can even initiate "conversations." They can "tell" you they saw a dog or an airplane and that they want you to pay attention to it. Parents say they never realized how many airplanes flew overhead until they taught their babies that specific sign.

Language Benefits

When you sign with your baby, you spark their language ability. A baby's first sign stimulates their interest in two-way communication and motivates them to also perfect their skills with the spoken word.

Another relevant finding in the Acredolo–Goodwyn study was that boys use signs as much as girls do. When it comes to language development, boys are usually slower to speak. But even though boys are gaining signing abilities, girls still tend to speak earlier than boys. Why is that? One popular theory is that mothers speak more to their daughters than to their sons.

Some other language benefits include:

- **Early communication.** Your baby has the ability to understand what you're saying long before their muscles enable them to respond. Once sign language bridges that gap, they won't have to wait to let you know you're not living up to their expectations. They can start critiquing you—and saying "I love you"—right now.

- **Earlier speech.** If you're concerned that sign language will delay your baby's spoken language development, worry not. Just the opposite is true. It's been shown that babies who sign speak earlier than those who don't. Signing won't stifle your baby's speech development. It actually helps babies learn to talk.

- **Larger vocabulary.** By the time a signing baby reaches the toddler stage, they have about 50 more spoken words than a nonsigning tyke. At three, they'll speak and understand at a four-year-old level. But because we all know that *your* child's not average, who knows what and how much they'll be saying!

Cognitive Benefits

When you sign with your baby, you get a child who speaks earlier and is more emotionally secure. But the cognitive benefits don't stop there. Some other advantages include:

- **Greater brain function.** Research on the brain has uncovered some amazing facts. Here's one of them: Spoken language is stored in the left side of the brain. Information obtained visually is stored in the right side. Because signing involves spoken language and eye involvement, both sides of the brain are used. Simply put, signing will help build more of your baby's brain and greater brain function.

- **Higher IQ.** Of course, nothing can be 100% guaranteed, but research indicates that babies who sign have higher IQs than babies who don't. Researchers Acredolo and Goodwyn give them as much as a 12-point advantage. While creating a smarter baby shouldn't be the primary reason to sign with your baby, don't ignore this benefit. Keep in mind, though, that IQ measures someone's ability to learn, not how smart someone is.

- **Higher reading level.** Because one way to reinforce the signs you'll teach your baby is with books, your baby will look forward to using them more interactively. In fact, research shows that signing children read at a higher level than nonsigners. Such an immediate and long-term cognitive benefit deserves attention.

What's in It for Parents?

Along with all the aforementioned benefits for your child are the personal rewards:

- You'll enjoy earlier and more meaningful interactions with your baby. Think how amazing and how much fun it'll be to see the world from their perspective.

- Your anxiety level will plummet. No need to guess where it hurts or what your baby wants when they're upset. Their signs will provide you with specific information about what's going on. That will make both of you feel better.

- One of the causes of tantrums and other negative behavior, such as biting or kicking, is a child's inability to communicate. When they can't express themselves, life can seem more challenging—for both of you. However, your child will have the ability to sign and can revert to signing when words fail them or emotions prevent speech.

- When you include grandparents and babysitters in the signing experience, they'll have an easier, more enjoyable time with your baby when you're not there. This further increases all the benefits of teaching sign language to your baby.

- Experience more peace and quiet. Less crying will happen once your baby learns that signing gets better and faster results than other attention-seeking actions. You'll also have peace of mind knowing you can understand each other.

- You'll have the knowledge that you've given your baby a gift that lasts a lifetime—and a head start in learning a second language: ASL.

Bragging About Your Bilingual Baby

The signs you'll teach your baby are based on authentic ASL. While some baby sign language programs suggest you make up your own signs or use a combination of homemade signs and ASL, your best bet is going with the real thing. Even if you only use sign language as a way to communicate with your baby before they actually talk, why not use elements of a real language? Who knows, you might want to continue your baby's sign language education beyond their early years. Then you can brag to your friends about having a bilingual child. Of course, there's a more practical reason to teach ASL to your baby: It's a standard language that others outside your family can understand.

Decades of research tells us that the period during the first two years of a baby's life is the crucial time to expose them to a second language—whether ASL or a foreign language. Remember that sign language is a step on the journey to spoken communication. But the time to plan is now. Sign language is a great beginning toward learning any language.

Chapter

Why and How It Works

Throughout the centuries, the brain has been a riddle to scientists. Ancient Greeks were convinced that the lungs directed our thoughts, feelings, and emotions. And if you lived in the 18th century, "experts" would analyze your skull to find out what was going on in your brain. If you had large temples, you'd have a talent for music. And certain characteristics at the base of your skull told them whether you'd make a good parent.

Even today, some questions about the brain go unanswered. However, modern techniques have turned up some pretty amazing facts about the brain and, in particular, how it develops. What they've found puts an even greater responsibility on parents: The experiences you give your baby during their early years have a *profound* influence on how their brains will develop and their future learning abilities.

Making Connections

When a baby's born, they have about 100 billion nerve cells. According to neurologists, they won't grow any new ones—ever. If that's the case, then how does a baby's brain grow after birth? By increasing the number of connections (synapses) between the neurons within their brain.

Each neuron is like a tiny octopus with thousands of tentacles. They carry signals that allow us to hear, see, taste, feel, move, remember, and think. It's where a baby stores information. A baby arrives with a limited number of these responses intact. They're only capable of hearing, feeling, sucking, and seeing in black and white. But within just a few days, their brain begins to analyze the outside world. With every experience, with their or your every touch, with every single sound they hear, another connection in their brain is made. The more connections, the more the baby's capable of complex thinking.

A baby's biologically primed for learning. By age three, a child's brain has twice as many synapses as an adult's. When those connections are used repeatedly in the early years, they become permanent. If not, they don't survive.

Brain Development

Aren't Mom and Dad's genes responsible for current and future brain development? Not totally, say the experts. In fact, your genes only determine your baby's main circuitry—those that control basic functions, such as breathing, heartbeat, and reflexes. That means trillions of connections will be determined by the stimulation you give your child throughout their early years.

The more you offer your child in the way of sensory and educational experiences, the more powerful their brain will become. This is an amazing thought. Not only will these experiences change the physical structure of your baby's brain, but they'll have a major impact on their intellectual and emotional well-being throughout their entire life.

How to Best Boost Your Baby's IQ

Current research is taking a second look at how effective developmental products are. They can be entertaining for sure, but can they build a better brain? Not without person-to-person interaction. That means that all the CDs and DVDs and online programs that claim to boost a baby's IQ only work when Mom and Dad get personally involved in presenting them.

Some obvious ways to interact with your baby are to read, sing, and talk to them as well as cuddle with them. But you can also help strengthen those mental connections by adding visual information—which is where sign language comes in.

The Sign Language Connection

When you sign with your baby, you're building additional connections in their brain. You're providing them with information that is or will be meaningful and you're repeating it and reinforcing the message. Every time you speak and sign with your baby, another brain connection is created. Exactly how does it work? How does sign language stimulate a baby's brain?

The left hemisphere of the brain is stimulated by the words you say when you sign. The right side receives and stores the visual information (signs) you present to your baby. You're thus engaging both sides of your baby's brain and increasing their chances of success—with sign language and other brain development.

In fact, when it comes to brain development, if a baby's rarely spoken to during their early years, they'll likely have difficulty mastering language skills. While a baby needs access to as much language as possible during the first three years, it needs to be direct, personal communication. It needs to be interactive.

This is where the use of hands becomes an important factor in brain development. When your baby's doing something with their hands, that means they're stimulating their brain with kinetic information and developing their fine motor skills at the same time. Simply put, signing with your baby is a multisensory experience—and an effective way to build more of their brain.

It's All in the Timing

Given what you now know, it shouldn't come as a surprise that babies and young children learn more in their first five years than they will during the rest of their lives. Because most of the wiring or connections in the brain happen

during that time, you have a small window of opportunity to make the most impact. And here's something else you need to know: There are critical windows for developing a baby's potential within that larger five-year window.

A dramatic example is visual development. If a baby isn't seeing the world around them normally by around six months, their vision might never be normal. Equal stimulation through both eyes is so important that if a baby with cataracts doesn't have them removed by six months, the risk for ongoing visual impairment or permanent blindness is extraordinarily high.

And then there's a baby's ability to learn language. The critical stage? Birth to age three. The more language that's presented to them during those years, the better their vocabulary and language skills will be throughout childhood and even into their adult life. Because experts tell us that parents who sign with their babies tend to talk to them more, your baby will be bombarded with visual and aural stimuli—another reason to sign.

When to Introduce Signs

Although many variables exist for knowing the best time to begin signing with your baby, because children acquire language naturally when it's present in their environment, you can really begin to sign anytime. In fact, it can be really beneficial to begin signing with your child as soon as you begin to speak to your baby—which is right from birth.

This can help babies begin to make associations. They start to understand that vocalizing gives them power. They make a sound and you come running. They can begin to realize that signing is also powerful—and that it's much more effective than crying.

A baby learns that when they cry, you'll appear, but you might not give them what they want—at least not immediately. However, when they sign, they discover they get much better results. The key to success, though, is through repetition, which helps your baby remember the signs and connect them with actions. They'll benefit from seeing signs well before they have the motor skills to imitate or reproduce those signs. All babies are different. While seven months might be the average age that most babies are first ready to reproduce signs, not all babies that age will be. Some will be at the starting gate at 6 months; others, not until 10 months to a year. How can you tell when the time is right for your future signer? Watch how they manipulate toys, and even more importantly, look for clues that they're interested in communicating.

Your baby's brain cells will grow and establish stronger connections when they're exercised. Sign language is a way to help strengthen the synapses and neural circuitry of your baby's brain. With this in mind, how would you answer the following questions?

- Does your baby look at your face intently when you speak?

- When your baby drops an object, do they look to see where it went?

- Does your baby seem really curious? For example, are they turning their head to see what's going on around them?

- When your baby picks up an object, do they look to you quizzically as if they're asking for more information?

- Does your baby point to the objects they want?

- Is your baby already gesturing on their own? For example, are they reaching out to be picked up or waving "bye-bye"?

- Can your baby imitate others' gestures or actions?

If you answered "yes" to five out of seven questions, then it's time to start teaching signing. If you answered "no" to the majority of the questions, wait a few weeks and review them again. Because babies are making major strides quickly at this stage, a few weeks can make all the difference. In the meantime, repeated exposure to signs as you speak will help your baby make those connections and build a memory bank of these new "gestures."

Manual Dexterity

Want another tip to help determine if your baby's nearing the signing stage? Look at their hands. Because a baby's hands must be agile enough to make the signs you're showing, this is another factor to consider. While there are numerous resources available about a baby's developmental stages, there's hardly any focus on how a baby's hands develop. Here's some general information on hand development:

- **2 months:** Their hands start to unfold and briefly hold a rattle.

- **3 months:** They play with their hands and can hold the rattle a little longer.

- **4 months:** They reach for objects.

- **5 months:** They grab their toes. Their reach is more accurate and they can transfer objects from hand to hand.

- **6–9 months:** They can pick up small objects with their thumb and finger. They reach accurately. Hands begin to meet at midline, like clapping.

- **12–15 months:** They can grip a crayon. This dexterity is indicative of more signs they'll be able to produce.

Jump-Starting the Process

If you've discovered your baby isn't quite ready to begin learning sign language, why not put the wait time to good use? Start learning the signs yourself, teach them to your family, and be ready when your child is.

Want to do even more? Try some simple activities to stimulate your baby's interest in sign language, improve their motor skills, and promote their spoken language development:

- Gently manipulate your baby's hands to help them with tasks they're having trouble with.

- Place Cheerios on their tray one at a time.

- Clap to music and songs. Gently take your baby's hands and help them with the movements and gestures.

- Play sorting games. Yes, you'll have to do most of the work, but speak as you play and explain your reasoning to your baby throughout the activity.

- Take your baby to a mirror and play "Identification." Touch your nose and say "This is Daddy's nose." Then touch your baby's nose and say "This is your nose." Then move on to your mouth, eyes, etc.

- Stimulate your baby with "touch and feel" activities. Present them with a number of different textures and let them feel the difference. For example, rub a silk scarf on their hand or let them feel a scrub brush (albeit gently).

- Get out a bubble wand and help them move their arm to create bubbles.

- Encourage them to move an object from one hand to the other.

- Make use of developmental toys with dials, cranks, buttons, and little doors.

- Read to your baby as often as possible. Because babies love repetition, limit the number of books you read to them. Take their finger and help them point to the objects/characters while stressing the name of each. If you know the sign for a word you're reading, show your baby that too while saying the word.

- Play Peek-a-Boo. This simple activity is great for developing and maintaining eye contact. That's important when it comes to signing.

When to Expect Results

How soon will you see results? There are variables you need to consider. It depends on how old your baby is and how regularly you sign with them, among other things.

While there are no crystal balls in this area, the following timetable will help give you a general idea of what to expect and when to expect it. Again, let me stress that this is based on an average and might not apply in all cases. Don't be discouraged if your baby doesn't follow this timetable—their personalities also come into play here. But you might even be surprised to see signs emerging sooner if you're consistent with their use.

- **3 to 6 months:** While babies are too young to begin any serious signing, this is a good time for you to put your baby in training and jump-start the process. Plus, it's a great time for you to practice what you're about to teach.

- **6 to 8 months:** Your baby's memory skills are growing daily. If you begin signing when your baby's in this age range, you could see results about two months later. This is based on a high level of commitment and consistency.

- **8 to 10 months:** Your baby's coordination skills have improved dramatically and they'll be able to produce simple signs and begin to grasp their meaning. If you start at this stage, you could see results in six to eight weeks.

- **10 to 12 months:** If you introduce signs to your baby at this age, you could see results in two to three weeks—even faster if you're using the express method detailed in Chapter 5.

- **12 to 18 months:** This is a prime imitation period. Watch what you say and watch what you sign. It could be picked up instantly, although the realization of what you're doing and why you're doing it might take a few days to a week.

Signing Variables

Why can't I be more exact? Because we're dealing with living human beings, too many variables exist that need to be considered:

- **Your baby's age:** The older the baby, the faster they'll sign.

- **What else is on their mind:** If your baby's learning to crawl or walk, that could delay things for a while. Babies under nine months are still trying to control their arms and legs. They'll learn to sign eventually, but they can only do so much all at once. Be patient. You might even see them stop signing something they were using well in order to focus on their physical growth, but the signs will come back.

- **Your baby's mood and interest level:** Your baby might not be interested in what you're teaching them. Try other signs. They know you'll eventually give them milk even if they don't make the request. They might just be more interested in the sign for DOG or DADDY. Or maybe they're just distracted at that moment.

- **Your commitment level:** The more committed you are to the concept of signing, the faster your baby will begin.

- **Your consistency level:** The more you sign with your baby, the faster they'll catch on.

- **Your family's involvement level:** The more family members who get involved, the quicker the results.

Rather than worry about when your baby will sign, try to have fun with the process. Until your baby shows you that first "sign" of progress, it might seem a bit repetitive. But repetition is how your baby will learn. However, the problem with repetition is that it's often accompanied by boredom. You can avoid this by teaching signs in myriad ways: as you talk, sing, read, play, etc.

Don't Give Up!

Keep in mind that your baby's benefitting from a language-rich environment. With signing, you're providing visual and aural stimulation, along with increased eye contact and face-to-face time. Your baby will also have time to watch your mouth move all day. It's possible your little one might not be an active signer but could still develop a solid vocabulary once they begin to speak. This time together can have tremendous benefits you might not recognize until much later.

Part

2

Ready, Set, Sign!

Signing with your baby should feel as natural as speaking to them. In this section, you'll learn how to get started with teaching baby sign language to your child. You'll also discover two methods you can use: a traditional approach and an express version.

Introducing Baby's First Signs

Now that you've decided to teach sign language to your baby, you need to make a choice about which method to use. Learning about the two main approaches should give you even more confidence that teaching sign language to your child is the right decision for their cognitive development.

Traditional Method vs. Express Method

You first need to determine if you want to use the traditional method or the express method. This really depends on your lifestyle and time constraints. Your baby will learn to sign regardless of which method you use.

The difference, though, is in the timing. With the express program, which is described in Chapter 5, your baby should be 11 months or older and you'll need to put in an intensive two-week effort to see results at the end of those two weeks. The traditional method, which is described in this chapter, takes a more relaxed approach. You can start when your baby's as young as six months, with results that could emerge two to three months later.

Take a look at the express program in the next chapter. See if that sounds right for you and your family. Then you can make the decision to start at six months or wait until 11 months. Or you can start slowly now, and if you're not seeing the results you'd hoped for, you can always change methods. Because all the techniques described in this chapter also work for the express program, feel free to use them regardless of which approach you take.

Sign Language Categories

Two types of signs you'll teach your baby:

- **Iconic signs:** These mimic the action or the look of what you're trying to communicate. Iconic signs are the easiest for you to teach and for your baby to learn. For example, you probably already know how to make the iconic sign for TELEPHONE: Your thumb to your ear and your pinkie finger to your mouth.

- **Abstract signs:** These are a little harder to teach because their meanings can't be conveyed by a simple gesture. To teach them, you'll need to create an association so your baby will make the connection. It sounds more complicated than it is. You'll understand better in our first example: the sign for MORE.

The First Three Signs: MORE, EAT, and MILK

I recommend teaching MORE, EAT, and MILK first because they're important concepts to your little one. In fact, in the earliest stages, they're pretty much all they care about. They want something to eat, something to wash it down with, and more of both. Another reason they work well is that none of them look alike. They won't confuse your baby—or you.

MORE is the sign that will serve as the foundation for all others. Once your baby understands this concept and can make the sign (or even come close), the other signs will come quickly. For those reasons, I'll spend more time on this sign and provide you with a greater number of examples. Of course, you're free to come up with your own.

The Sign for MORE

Even though it's an abstract concept, MORE is a sign babies learn very quickly. Oftentimes, it's their very first spoken word. It's also a good starter sign because there are many different opportunities to teach it throughout the day. In other words, you won't get bored.

Your baby can use this sign to ask for more food, more juice, or more pages of the book you're reading to them. All they have to do is put their fingertips together and "ask."

Put your fingertips together a few times.

Techniques to Teach MORE

- When you're feeding your baby, give them a few teaspoons from that jar of green beans or whatever the "daily special" might be. Then pause. Before they can get upset, make the sign for MORE and ask: "MORE? Do you want MORE?" Continue this during the meal, making sure there are enough "feeding stoppages" so the idea begins to register. Repeat this pattern frequently throughout every meal, stressing the word MORE while you sign. Use an expressive and upbeat tone of voice. Smile and make a game of it. Eventually, your baby will make the association if you keep repeating the routine. Like learning anything new, repetition is essential.

- Grab a handful of Cheerios. While your baby's in their high chair, put one on their tray. When they pick it up and pop it in their mouth, ask/sign "MORE?" Then quickly place another one in front of them. As soon as they eat it, be ready to have another one magically appear, remembering to reinforce the idea by signing and speaking every time.

- Read a book to your baby. (Babies love to hear your voice and look at the pictures no matter how young they are.) Stop at certain intervals, look at your baby, and ask/sign if they want MORE. Repeat this several times during the reading session, always asking in speech and sign "MORE? Do you want me to read MORE?"

- Play Peek-a-Boo. It's always a baby-pleaser. Stop every so often and ask/sign MORE. Then resume playing the game. Then do it again and again. And again.

- Play Baby Toss-Up. All babies love it. Pick them up and toss them gently in the air and wait for the belly laughs to begin. Then stop and ask if they want MORE. Repeat the activity.

- Put a rubber ducky in their bathtub and sink it. Then have it pop up. If they think it's funny, ask if they'd like MORE.

- Gather the family around the kitchen table, with your baby watching from their high chair or from someone's lap. Ask family members if they'd like MORE of something. Exaggerate the effort. Have them respond (and sign) that they would. Then place more on their plates.

When teaching MORE, be careful not to deprive your baby of food or anything else for too long a period. Your goal is to get them to make the connection between the sign for MORE and actually getting more of something they want. Learning has to be fun!

One idea that might help your baby make the connection is to recruit a favorite teddy bear or doll with moveable hands. Give teddy a cracker, pretend they ate it, and then ask if they'd like MORE. Then bring teddy's hands together, making the sign. Make sure your baby's watching the action. You might find that your baby's first attempts to sign MORE look like clapping or pointing one index finger in the opposite palm. Those are typical approximations and truly a great start! Give positive feedback and continue to model the actual sign.

Move your hand back and forth to your mouth as if you're holding a cracker and eating it.

The Sign for EAT

To learn how to sign EAT, your baby will have to make another association. But because the sign for EAT pantomimes someone actually eating something, it's one that's easy to teach and easy for everyone to remember.

Techniques to Teach EAT

- It's suppertime and your baby's in their high chair watching you prepare their food. You can tell by their behavior that they're excited about the prospect of eating. Sit down in front of them with a bowl of their favorite strained vegetables, and before you begin to feed them, ask/sign: "EAT? Would you like to EAT?" Again, keep your voice upbeat and make sure to smile. By the way, did you notice the difference between EAT and MORE?

With EAT, you make the sign several times before feeding your baby. Why? If you stop and start throughout the meal to teach the sign, your baby might get EAT and MORE confused. If your baby has already begun to sign MORE, they might use it to indicate a desire to eat but will likely add the new sign soon enough.

- You don't have to wait until your baby's in the high chair to help them make the association. When you get them out of their crib and dressed before breakfast, make the sign for EAT before you leave the room, asking them if they're hungry and ready to EAT their cereal. Then make sure you take them directly to the high chair so they make the connection. On your way there, ask/sign that same question a few more times. Remember to speak when you sign.

- Surprise your baby at other times of the day by asking them if they'd like something to EAT. Repeat the question a few times and then produce a cracker so the meaning is reinforced.

- Use whatever props you can think of to reinforce the sign and its association. For example, feed the dog or a family member or offer a pretend snack to a stuffed bear.

Your hand opens and closes as if you were milking a cow. Alternative: Many nursing moms use the sign for NURSE. It's made by quickly brushing your hand over your breast in a downward motion.

The Sign for MILK

When you introduce the sign for MILK, you have a different kind of association to make. MILK is something your baby can see and touch (a bottle or a breast).

Techniques to Teach MILK

- Before you give your baby their bottle or your breast, you'll ask/sign: "MILK? Would you like some MILK?" Follow the same method as with other signs, repeating the question a few times. Then give them the bottle or breast.

- During their feeding, while their attention is focused on you, reinforce the sign by asking/signing: "MILK?

Do you like MILK?" While it might be difficult to feed your baby and sign at the same time, ask your spouse or another family member to sign and say MILK/ NURSE while your baby eats, making sure they show the sign within your baby's sight line.

- If you begin signing with your baby while nursing or milk is their only meal, then this sign can come before EAT.

Teaching Other Important Signs

One of the reasons babies enjoy signing is it helps them feel good about themselves. They begin to gain a sense of independence. At last, they have some control over what's going on. I've already stated you should adapt these guidelines to meet your own goals, but here's a strong suggestion: In the beginning stages, teach your baby the signs they (and you) really need. In other words, teach them the following signs before you venture into the good manners and good grooming categories. You can always show them the sign for TOOTHBRUSH next week. However, if your pet dog or your baby's teddy bear feels as important as the need for MORE, those are good signs to also teach.

Bring the tips of your index fingers together a few times at the location of pain.

The Sign for HURT/PAIN

The sign for HURT/PAIN is one of the most important signs you can teach your baby. Once they learn this sign, not only can they tell you when they're in pain but also where it hurts. Instead of simply crying, your baby will have a valuable tool to help them communicate the source of their pain. They'll simply make the sign at the place on their body where it hurts. The bad news is that to learn the sign for HURT/PAIN, your baby must make the association between the sign and pain itself. Unfortunately, they'll have many opportunities to learn firsthand when they're crawling and starting to walk.

It doesn't matter what word you use: HURT, PAIN, BOO-BOO, and OW all work fine. Just remember that consistency is essential. If you're not too consistent, your baby will begin to learn synonyms—and that's also okay.

Techniques to Teach HURT/PAIN

- When your baby has stubbed their toe or bumped their head, give them some cuddles and comfort and, of course, make sure it's only a superficial injury. Then while you're soothing them, make the sign for HURT/PAIN where it hurts. For example, if they hurt their knee, make the sign in front of their knee, saying sympathetically: "Did you HURT yourself? Does it HURT? I'm sorry it HURTS." Remember to stress the word HURT each time, always signing at the point of pain.

- If the pain is outside your baby's line of vision (such as the nose or forehead), gently touch or rub the spot where they were hurt and then make the sign for HURT at that same location on your own body. Make sure they're paying attention and not still totally focused on their pain. Repeat this several times, talking to them soothingly. Another alternative is to take them to a mirror so they can see you make the sign at their own nose or forehead. That will help them make a more personal connection.

- Pretend to hurt yourself while your baby's watching. For example, bump your knee and then overreact by hopping around, gritting your teeth, and making the sign for HURT at your "injury."

- Use a teddy bear as a "crash dummy" and have them injure their head or paw. Then make the sign where they were hurt and maybe use a bandage for reinforcement.

Pat your chest with your palms open a few times.

The Sign for HELP

HELP is another sign you'll want your baby to learn. It can help eliminate some crying and frustration on your baby's part. You won't have to guess what's wrong with them when they start to cry.

Techniques to Teach HELP

- Look for situations where your child might actually need help. For example, they drop a toy from their crib. You come over and ask/sign: "HELP? Do you want HELP?" Then do whatever needs doing to rectify the situation.

- Watch your child at play. If you notice a moment where you think they might need help, ask/sign: "Do you need HELP?" If they indicate they don't, then back off. Remember, you're not only trying to teach them sign language, but you also want them to learn independence.

- Because situations where your baby needs help might not occur frequently enough for them to make the necessary association, you might need to create scenarios that allow you to teach this sign. Try to show this sign being performed in different places in your home.

All fingers except the thumbs curl into your palms. Your knuckles rest against each other and pivot in opposite directions. (The sign for DIAPER CHANGE is actually the sign for CHANGE, with DIAPER being implied.)

The Sign for DIAPER CHANGE

Can a baby really "tell" you when they need their diaper changed? With today's disposable diapers, your baby might not feel uncomfortable or mind being wet or messy.

But there are babies who abhor the feeling and would be thrilled to have an efficient way to call attention to this.

DIAPER CHANGE isn't as essential as other signs, but because it might benefit your baby, why not give it a try and see what happens? If your baby wakes up in the middle of the night soaked through, it could be a great way for you to know they're not hungry or in pain.

Techniques to Teach DIAPER CHANGE

When you introduce the sign for DIAPER CHANGE, your goal is to get your baby to communicate when they're uncomfortable and wants you to change their diaper. For your baby to make this association, they need to be aware of the process of having a diaper taken off and a new one put on. Your reactions when you actually change their diaper will help reinforce that awareness.

- When a baby has a wet or soiled diaper, make a big deal about changing it. Because the sign requires two hands, put your baby on a blanket on the floor or some other safe place. Then say/sign: "DIAPER CHANGE? Do you need a DIAPER CHANGE?" Repeat this a few times, making sure you stress the words DIAPER CHANGE as well as the sign.

- Remove your baby's diaper while saying/signing something like "You really needed a DIAPER CHANGE!" or "A DIAPER CHANGE is my favorite thing to do."

- Once the diaper is off and your baby's clean, place a diaper behind you or somewhere out of your baby's sight. Then say/sign "Where's the DIAPER?" Pretend to look around you while asking the same question. Keep repeating it and signing. Then magically bring the diaper into your baby's sight line as you enthusiastically say/sign "Here's the DIAPER! We found the DIAPER!"

- You can also diaper a teddy bear or a baby doll to help your baby make the association. In fact, using an inanimate object works well for teaching many signs.

Looking for Signs of Progress

What do you do if you've been signing for a month or two and nothing's happening? If you think your baby should be making better progress (based on all the variables we discussed earlier), here are some things you can do to determine if you're making any headway:

- Say a target word (MORE, EAT, etc.) without making the sign. Pay close attention to see if your baby's eyes travel down to your hands. If so, it means they're used to receiving information orally and visually. You're definitely making progress.

- Place your baby's bottle on the floor with a few other objects. Then watch them carefully as you sign and say MILK. If they look to the bottle, you're really

getting close. Try the same thing with a diaper, a book, or other object signs you're trying to teach.

- Keep in mind that your idea of progress might not be the same as your baby's. Their signs might not look like yours at first. It takes lots of dexterity to make some of them perfectly. In fact, your baby might already be signing and you might not even know it.

Recognizing Early Attempts

How will you be able to figure out what your baby's trying to sign to you in the beginning stages? While their signs might not replicate yours exactly, they're doing their best and need acknowledgment for their efforts.

Look for any motions or gestures that seem out of the ordinary, especially if your baby keeps repeating them. If you still can't figure out what your baby's trying to communicate, look around. Chances are it has something to do with the current situation or a nearby object. If you're still not sure, it might help to know more about the first attempts of other babies:

- **MORE:** Some babies clap their hands together. Others close their fists and tap them together when they want MORE of something.

- **EAT:** There are babies who put their hand or fist in their mouth or point to their mouth with one finger when they want something to EAT.

- **MILK:** A thirsty baby might wave or shake their hand or even reach out toward their bottle or your breast for MILK.

When your baby approximates a sign, show them you're pleased with the effort, but then demonstrate the correct way to do it. Don't imitate their attempt. As your baby's fine motor skills improve, so will their ability to make the sign properly. Do what you can to identify what your baby's trying to communicate to you. Once you do, lavish them with praise while showing the correct sign.

Ten Signing Suggestions

Follow these recommendations to help you achieve signing success:

- Always sign in context.

- Once you begin to sign in a certain situation, continue.

- Remember to speak as you sign.

- Use body language along with maximum facial and vocal expressions.

- Encourage a reluctant child to sign by occasionally (and gently) shaping their hands into a sign.

- Reward your child's efforts—even if they just come close and approximate a sign. Cheer them on!

- Use any and all creative ways you can to reinforce signs.

- Never show disappointment or express any negative reactions if your baby doesn't sign or mixes them up.

- Have patience! Don't expect instant results with every sign.

- Make the sign language experience meaningful and fun!

The Express Version

If you're looking for the fastest way to communicate with your hearing baby through sign language, this chapter is for you. There are two major components you'll need to be successful in this venture: One is a baby who's 11 months or older and the other is 2 weeks you can devote to this version. For this method to work, you need to make signing a primary focus in your household. Plus, you'll need the help of anyone else who comes in contact with your baby. Think of this as a sign language immersion program.

Teaching a baby sign language is pretty standard regardless of the approach. This express program consolidates and accelerates the experience with additional awareness opportunities in a more concentrated period of time.

How Soon Can You Expect Results?

When you sign with your baby using the traditional method discussed in Chapter 4, you start when your baby's as young as six or seven months and you might see results in two months. With the express version, if your baby's 11 months or older and you follow this two-week program, you might see results in two weeks or less. That's right: You might see results before you've completed the program.

What's the Big Deal About 11 Months?

At 11 months, most babies are developmentally ready to appreciate signing and will grasp the concept more quickly. They also have enough manual dexterity to mimic the gestures and sufficient brain power to remember the signs. Will some babies have those skills earlier than 11 months? Yes. But if you're looking to see quick results, this method will help with that.

Another reason why 11 months is such an important benchmark is that it's closer to the period when you and your baby will get the most out of sign language. Frustration because of limited communication skills reaches its peak between 12 and 24 months. When you give your baby the ability to communicate—even on a very basic level—you're giving them a vital tool to express themselves.

There's one exception to the 11-month rule. Let's say you started signing with your baby when they were six months old and you

incorporated sign language into your daily routine. Now it's three months later and your baby isn't "getting it." In that case, try the express method. It will speed things up. In other words, if you've been signing for at least three months and you're getting discouraged, try this version. Just remember to adapt the guidelines to your own baby and lifestyle.

Why the Big Rush?

The number one reason babies don't sign is because parents lose their enthusiasm and quit. Perhaps they started too early, expected too much too soon, or just didn't have the time or patience to follow through. But this express method can help parents who are looking for more immediate results.

Can I guarantee that your baby will sign in two weeks? No. But I can guarantee that if you stick with the program and follow my suggestions, your baby will sign as fast as they can. I encourage you to enjoy the experience of teaching your baby to sign—and you'll be thrilled when that happens.

Step-by-Step Express Method

You have two weeks to do a lot of work and make your baby a more active communicator in the family. That's your mission. To accomplish it, you need a strategy that's meaningful and fun—and one that fully immerses your baby in the sign language experience.

Step 1: Circle the Calendar

Decide on a two-week period of time when you feel you can devote most of your energies to teaching your baby to sign. Double-check your calendar to make sure no other major commitments require extensive planning or will take up a large chunk of your time. Of course, everyday things still have to occur, but it's important to keep your signing awareness level as high as possible. Whenever you spend time with your baby within that two-week period, you have to think "sign language."

Step 2: Do Your Homework

Rather than repeating what I've written elsewhere, I'm going to refer you to other chapters for helpful hints and advice. While you might not be interested in the history and science behind teaching a hearing baby to sign, Chapter 4 is mandatory. In the express method, because we're going to be using those same techniques, it's vital information. So are the "Ten Signing Suggestions" at the end of that chapter. Think of them as success tips rather than actual commands.

To keep your motivational level elevated, Chapter 2 discusses all the benefits of signing with your baby. Glance at it over the two-week period. It will keep you going.

Step 3: Do Some Handiwork

You don't need to wait until you've completed steps 1 and 2 to undertake this component of the plan. Start right now to do whatever you can to bring focus and attention to your fingers and hands. Your goal is to make your baby

aware of their hands and realize what fun it is to have a matching pair.

Also, concentrate on your baby's fine motor skills using visual and tactile reinforcement. Let them see you do interesting or even crazy things with your hands. Then take their hands and see if you can get them to duplicate those activities. But remember, this has to be fun for your baby. Chances are they'll love the "games" and think of you as the best playdate they've ever had. (Revisit Chapter 3 for other ways to jump-start the process.) Get creative and come up with games and activities that will get your baby to pay attention to their and your hands. Here are a few ideas:

- Dance, wave your hands above your head, and move your fingers.

- Hide your face behind open fingers. Open and close them to play Peek-a-Boo.

- Draw a little face on your thumbs and let your thumbs have a "conversation."

- Wave "bye-bye" every time someone leaves the house—or even leaves a room. Wave as a car passes. Gently take your baby's hand and help them wave if they're having trouble.

- Play music and clap loudly to the beat. Take your baby's hands and clap for them.

Step 4: Recruit Your Volunteers

Set up a meeting with siblings, grandparents, caregivers, and anyone else who comes into daily contact with your child. If they know little or nothing about signing, give them the benefit of your knowledge (and mine) and talk to them about how much this will benefit your baby and how important their participation is. Then explain what will happen and their vital role in the success of the two-week venture. This is especially important if they have older children—the best teachers of all. They'll love being included and thrilled to teach your littlest one to sign. It makes them feel important and special. If your child spends time in daycare or with another caregiver, involve them in the process. Keeping everyone informed and updated speeds progress and enables everyone to feel good about what they're doing.

Week 1: Introducing the First Sign

The first sign you'll teach is for MORE. As the illustration shows, to make the sign, the fingertips of one hand come in contact with the fingertips of the other. MORE is an important sign—not only because it's the first one you'll introduce but because it's the sign that will trigger awareness that gestures have meaning. So don't think of it as teaching a sign but rather teaching its association.

The general concept is to identify something your baby really enjoys, then stop during the activity and ask if they want you to continue—always orally stressing the word "more." "MORE? Would you like MORE?" Repeat the question with the sign a few times during each activity. After you ask the question, wait a few seconds as if you're expecting a response. Then give them more of what they want—before they get angry or frustrated.

For your baby to "get it," vary the signing contexts. Don't just use MORE at mealtime—use it throughout the entire day in as many circumstances you can think of. More books, more Peek-a-Boo, more silly games. Keep asking them if they want MORE. Keep in mind that once you start signing in a particular situation, continue to do it. Repetition is the key to enlightenment. Check out Chapter 4 for some ways to help your baby make the association. Get creative and find what your baby likes best.

Week 2: Staying Focused and On Track

You made it through the first week. You've been signing MORE to your baby and repeating the activities whenever possible. Your family members have been doing the same thing. Your babysitter has joined you in the effort. What do you do now? Relax.

Take a deep breath. You had a great week, right? Everyone takes this subject so seriously. You can't really make a mistake as long as you have your baby's best interest at heart. So keep going. Success is only one hand signal away.

At the beginning of the second week, start paying closer attention to your baby. You'll probably notice they'll be paying more attention to their hands and yours—and maybe playing with their own hands more often than they usually do. During this time, they might also make their first sign—or attempt to test it out and see if anyone's paying attention.

It's important to be aware of the fact that your baby's initial attempts at making the sign for MORE might not be as perfect as your own. They might clap, touch one finger to their palm, or open and close their fingers. Regardless of how your baby makes the sign for MORE, you should continue to produce it correctly. Don't adapt to their signing variations because they might change as time goes by. As they get older, your baby's signing proficiency will improve.

Keep in mind that signing activities should only occur when your baby's in a good mood and enjoying them. Forcing them to clap their hands when they want to rub their sleepy eyes will get you nowhere and could very well sabotage your efforts.

You might also find that your baby chooses to say the word instead of using the sign. By always using the word and sign together, you're giving them the option. In these cases, keep using the sign and repeating the word so your baby can perfect their pronunciation.

When Your Baby Makes Their First Sign

Many parents liken the day their baby makes their first sign to the day they said their first word or took their first step. It really is a thrill and something to record in their baby book. However, once you enter the event, it's time to get back to work. But it will get a little easier. When a baby makes their first sign, the others usually follow more quickly.

But just because your baby has made the sign for MORE, you can't cross that one off your lesson plan. It needs to be continually reinforced. It's the "Use it or lose it" theory. Use the sign as before in all the previous situations—and make sure when your baby signs for MORE that you give them more of what they want. Remember that you're reinforcing the association as well as the sign.

While reinforcing MORE, you're also going to teach two more signs: EAT and MILK.

No Sign of a Sign?

If you've yet to see progress, don't get discouraged. Your time will come. You're making progress even if your baby's hands are still stuck in their mouth. Remember that your baby's receptive abilities at this age far outshine their expressive skills. That means they're listening. They're paying attention. And they're just trying to determine what the best time will be for them to make their signing debut.

What you need to do now is exactly what you've been doing: Keep reinforcing the sign for MORE—and consider incorporating the

following attention-getters into your routine.
Your baby might just need some variety for
them to start signaling for attention.

- Vary the proximity of the sign. As long as
  you have eye contact with your baby, you
  can vary the distance.

- Touch or pat your baby's hand before you
  make the sign.

- Gently shape your baby's hands to make
  the sign—but don't force them to do it.

Even though your baby doesn't seem to have
a clue as to what's going on, after one week,
move forward. That's right. Even though you
might not have seen any visible progress, your
baby's paying close attention—and they're
ready to take in more than MORE. Now
you'll teach them EAT and MILK.

Introducing Additional Signs

Regardless of whether your baby's signing,
after one week of signing MORE, you're going
to introduce two new signs: EAT and MILK.
It's important you don't confuse the baby by
using all three signs at one time. For example,
introduce EAT by showing them a cracker and
asking if they want to EAT. Repeat that a few
times. After they wake up from a nap, ask if
they want MILK and show them their bottle.
Gradually bring all the signs together when
you can tell they're making the connections.
And don't forget MORE. You still need to
include that in your signing repertoire.

Introducing the Sign for EAT

Take a look at Chapter 4 for ways to proceed
with this sign. It's simply moving your hand
back and forth to your mouth as if you're
eating something. Pay particular attention to
the section about keeping the signs for MORE
and EAT distinct. Sign EAT before you put
your baby in the high chair. And never use the
signs MORE and EAT together because that
will result in obvious confusion.

Continue to use MORE in a wide variety of
contexts—not just when you're feeding your
baby. Your baby might confuse MORE with
EAT—or think it's the sign for the Cheerios
you're using to entice them.

Introducing the Sign for MILK

Open and close your fist as if you're milking
a cow. If you're breastfeeding and prefer to use
that sign, brush your hand lightly over your
breast in a downward motion.

While you should again refer to Chapter 4, you probably don't need too much explanation. By now, you realize that signing is a matter of presenting the sign in such a way that the association makes sense. With MILK, you have a natural way to reinforce that association. Simply make the sign several times as you're nursing or giving your baby their bottle.

Deciding Where to Go From Here

You can indeed stop once your baby masters all three signs. It isn't essential you do more. But why stop now? At the very least, keep signing until their speech takes center stage. Plus, signing will definitely help lower their frustration level if you send them out into the world equipped with a few signs. Some parents say they've almost become addicted to signing. Once they start, it becomes second nature. It's brought them and their family closer and has given the baby a more active role.

What Else Is There to Learn?

Your baby knows the signs, but they don't yet realize the power they have in their hands—quite literally. They're ready for a larger role so they can more fully convey their full range of emotions. There are so many signs still to learn: Signs they can combine, sentences they can make, thoughts they can convey, and questions they can pose. What happens when they do speak? Will they drop their signs altogether? Will they sign *and* speak? What about your role in the process? Chapter 8 answers those questions for you.

An Important Note for Parents-in-Waiting

Many of you have read this material and are thinking about waiting for your baby's 11-month birthday. If that's the case, don't just sit around watching the calendar. Put the time to good use. Here are a number of things you can do to promote signing readiness as you count down to the big day:

- Read this book from cover to cover and get ready for signing day. Practice the signs you'll be introducing.

- Play the manual dexterity "games" discussed in Chapter 3.

- Continue to read and talk to your child. That will not only help with signing but also with speech language development.

- Remember, you can always start using the traditional method if your baby's at least six months old.

Chapter

Increasing Your Baby's Sign Language Vocabulary

If you taught your baby all the signs in Chapter 5, you don't really have to go any further. Many parents are content with just providing the basic signs. If you decide to stop now, you and your baby will still reap many of the rewards discussed earlier. However, you'll miss out on even greater benefits and lots more fun. To that end, this chapter will help you extend your baby's signing vocabulary.

Some signs are more important to parents and caregivers than they are to babies. DON'T TOUCH and GENTLE TOUCH are two of them. While your baby might not sign them, understanding them can be essential.

The Sign for DON'T TOUCH

DON'T TOUCH is a combination of the sign for NO and the sign for TOUCH. As you might imagine, once your baby begins to roam, DON'T TOUCH is a sign you'll use frequently. Will it help them communicate their wants and needs? No, it won't. But you want to keep your baby safe, which means teaching DON'T TOUCH can help you add emphasis to your oral instructions. Elevator buttons, electrical outlets, bugs, and dirty diapers are just a few things you might want to keep your baby from touching—and with this sign, you can help them learn the concept.

Techniques for DON'T TOUCH

- Like with any other sign, your baby needs to make an association. When you see them touching something they shouldn't, quickly grab their hand, make eye contact, and show them the sign while shaking your head and sternly saying "DON'T TOUCH." This won't be your baby's favorite sign, but it will help you keep them out of harm's way. Just remember the four components that are necessary to get your message across: the tone of your voice, your stern facial expression, your spoken words, and the sign itself.

DON'T TOUCH is a combination of NO and TOUCH. Your index and middle fingers snap to the thumb (NO) and then your middle finger taps the back of the other hand (TOUCH).

- Spread some objects in a row on the floor. It doesn't matter what they are, but one should be different from the rest. For example, line up some of your baby's picture books and one of your own thick best sellers. Or try five stuffed toys and one wooden one. Then touch each object, saying with a happy voice and a smile: "Touch. Touch. Touch. Touch. Touch." When you get to your book, begin to touch it, but then quickly pull your hand away. At the same time, make a noticeable frown and say in a much deeper voice "DON'T TOUCH!" and make the sign. Vary the sequence so the "untouchable" object isn't always last. After you do this a few times, take your baby's hand and gently guide them through the same activity. If you play this "game" enough, your baby will make the association. Choose objects they really shouldn't touch and remember it's for your baby's safety.

- Walk your baby around the kitchen, touching different things while happily saying: "Touch. Touch. Touch." When you get to the stove or toaster, begin to reach out to touch them, then quickly pull your hand away, lower your voice, make a stern face, and say/sign "DON'T TOUCH!" This activity should be "played" more seriously than the previous version using the books or toys, as these are objects that are potentially much more dangerous and you *really* don't want your baby to touch them.

One hands gently "pets" the back of the other hand.

The Sign for GENTLE TOUCH

Another valuable sign is GENTLE TOUCH. Basically, it's one hand "petting" the back of the other hand, as if you were stroking a cat. And speaking of cats, that's one of the reasons this sign is important. If you have a cat or another pet or are visiting a friend who has one, your baby's first inclination might be to grab or squeeze it. With the GENTLE TOUCH sign, you can teach them to be kind and gentle in their manner of touch. The soothing tone of your voice as you "pet" your hand will help convey its meaning. The sign is also useful when holding delicate objects or when visiting friends with babies younger than yours. Doing the sign on your baby's hand can further demonstrate the meaning of the sign.

Techniques for GENTLE TOUCH

- Rub their arm or leg while saying slowly and soothingly: "GENTLE TOUCH. GENTLE TOUCH."

- Use a teddy bear or a family volunteer. While your baby's watching, rub the subject's arm while speaking and signing "GENTLE TOUCH."

- If you have a pet, caress it gently, guiding your baby's hand over its fur while saying and signing "GENTLE TOUCH."

Where to Go From Here

Although the methods won't get easier, results will come through patience, practice, and commitment. It might help before you determine the next step to ask yourself what you're trying to accomplish and set some goals.

Do you want your baby to become skilled in sign language and use it into early childhood—maybe even as an adult? If that's your goal, keep in mind that this is baby sign language and it's as basic as it gets. It's a way for a child to communicate what they want and feel in a very limited way. While this is a great place to start, if you're really serious about teaching sign language as a second language, a more comprehensive and structured approach is necessary and a Deaf teacher or native speaker of ASL can be your best teacher.

However, if you're like many hearing parents and want to use sign language solely as a communication bridge before your baby can express themselves with speech, you'll want to decide which signs to teach after you've introduced the basics.

To help you establish your signing goals, ask yourself which signs would be most helpful to your baby in expressing themselves. Consider your daily routines and your baby's favorite things. Also, ask what would be helpful to you in understanding what they want or feel. And don't forget the fun factor! Think about what signs your baby could learn just for the sheer delight of it.

To help you decide, look at the signs in Appendix A. They're authentic ASL signs and are the most popular with parents because they're all relevant to a baby's world. Review the different categories and decide which ones you'd like your baby to learn. Regardless of your decisions, keep in mind that the goals you set are simply guidelines to help you establish some direction. Keep them flexible. You'll soon learn why.

Introducing Additional Signs

Perhaps your baby has mastered the basics. They've come to realize that gestures have meaning. They know that when they make a particular sign, they get an object or a response they want. By now, you've reviewed all the signs and have decided which signs you want to add to your baby's signing vocabulary. But how and when do you teach them?

How would you go about introducing new spoken words to your child's vocabulary? Hard to put into words, isn't it? That's because teaching your baby to speak is something that just comes naturally. You talk, your baby listens, and they imitate what they hear. If your baby sees something they're interested in, they'll stare at it, pick it up, or point to it. You react by slowly saying the name of whatever they're interested in and repeating the word so they remember it. Teaching your baby new signs isn't that different. The only change is that when you say the word, you add a sign. All it takes is your memory and a keen eye.

Identifying Signing Opportunities

Let's say you've decided to teach your baby all the signs in the clothing category. Keeping in mind they must make an association before they can learn any of them, when do you think the ideal time would be to teach them? Of course—when you're getting them dressed in the morning and undressed at night. Going for a walk outside? Teach them the signs for SHOES, HAT, and COAT.

Interested in teaching your baby good manners? Mealtime would be a good place to start. What about animal signs? Use their favorite animal picture book. Analyze your daily routine. You're sure to discover many teaching opportunities right in front of you, such as BATH, CHANGE, and SLEEP.

The important thing to remember is to make your teaching relevant. Always sign in context. It's critical that your baby associate meaning to the signs you're showing them. And because they won't figure it all out immediately, you need to make the signs and reinforce their associations repeatedly.

Creating Your Own Opportunities

A major resource is available to you when it comes to introducing and reinforcing signs you want your baby to learn. It's something that's jam-packed with ongoing teaching opportunities. It's called life.

Look around you. Life is a signing classroom. Take your "student" on a few field trips. Even your backyard is an adventure to a baby. Just open the door and point to what you see, say the word, and make the sign. What about a trip to the zoo? What a great opportunity to teach animal signs! And what better way to teach family member signs than hauling out the family photo album?

Following Your Baby's Lead

Another way (and the best way) to figure out what signs to teach your baby is to take their lead. Yes, your baby can and will tell you what they want to learn if you pay attention.

Remember those goals you set several paragraphs ago and the advice to keep them flexible? That suggestion is because your baby might have a different signing philosophy than you do. For example, let's say you're sitting on a blanket in the backyard trying to teach your baby the sign for BOOK. Suddenly, they throw the book down, look up, and point to a bird. If that happens, it's a priceless opportunity to teach them a sign. In effect, they're saying: "I'm no longer intrigued by that book. But I'm really interested in that thing up there. What is it? Can you give me more information?" It's a perfect opportunity to keep your goals flexible and seize the moment. While signing BIRD, say: "Oh, a BIRD! Look at that beautiful BIRD. Look, there's another BIRD."

Being Prepared

To promote baby-driven signing opportunities, let your child explore. Be prepared with as many signs as you can. If they pick up a diaper, be ready with the sign for DIAPER CHANGE. If they pick up a sneaker, show them the sign for SHOE. If they point to the TELEPHONE, your baby wants to know more. That could be a good opportunity for a phone call or FaceTime with the grandparents. Give them more information. Tell them the name of an object and show them the sign.

Review the signs in Appendix A and practice those that are likely to come up. Because many of the signs are iconic—meaning they mimic the action or the look of what you're trying to communicate—you'll have an easy time remembering them. Learn a few more each day and you'll be an expert in no time.

But what happens if your baby picks something up and you don't know the sign? Don't panic! Other chances will happen. Just remember to look up that sign and be ready the next time.

But you can also do something else if you don't know a sign: Make one up. In Chapter 1, professors Acredolo and Goodwyn suggested you invent your own sign in a situation like that. Their advice is to create a simple gesture that represents the look or idea of the object. For example, if you don't know the sign for DOG, consider panting like one.

Whether you should follow that strategy depends on your overall objective. If you want your baby to take ASL seriously or if you find the bilingual benefits essential, then pass up the opportunity, look up the legitimate ASL sign, and be ready the next time. If your objective is shorter-term and you don't plan on teaching your baby any more signs after they learn to talk, then you might give it a try. However, it's important to remember that others might not be able to identify the signs you created on your own because they're not part of any standard sign language. And if you forget a sign you made up, you'll need to create a different one, which can cause confusion.

Your Baby's Own Inventions

In Chapter 1, you learned how Linda Acredolo became inspired to study this subject in the first place. If you recall, it was when her daughter Kate spontaneously began to make up her own signs. Her sign for FISH was to blow because there was a fish mobile over her crib and her mom had to blow on it to make it move. To Kate, sniffing and wiggling her nose meant FLOWER because she saw people doing something similar when they picked one from the garden.

What do you do if your baby makes up their own sign? Get excited, praise them for their creativity, and respond by giving them what they want or show you understand in some other way. But then you have to make another decision: Do you incorporate your baby's invented sign into your sign language lexicon or do you respond by showing them the actual sign you want them to learn? When you think about it, it's pretty much the same quandary you had when your baby asked you for a sign and you didn't know it. Again, it's really your call and depends on how much of an ASL purist you are and want your child to become.

One really important thing you need to keep in mind if you do opt to continue to use your baby's own signs: Record it somewhere and let your family and other caregivers know about it. Nothing will dampen your baby's enthusiasm for signing like not being understood by everyone. That said, continuing to model the actual sign can benefit your baby's language development in the long run. For example, when they request their "bah bah," you'd want them to hear the word "bottle" in return to fully develop the language.

This bears repeating: Teach sign language the same way you teach your baby to speak. You're not concerned about talking to your baby too much, are you? Do they understand every single word you say to them? Of course not, but that doesn't stop you from talking. In fact, the more you talk, the better their vocabulary will become. It's the same with signing.

Combining Signs

While putting more than one sign together isn't essential to your baby's signing success, if the opportunity presents itself, take advantage. Because you're speaking more than one-word thoughts, you can also model signing them.

Your baby might make combinations on their own. Maybe they'll sign MORE and MILK when they want a refill. Be prepared and be impressed when that happens.

If they don't combine signs on their own, offer some encouragement. EAT and MORE are a good starting combo. Just be certain your baby understands both signs and both concepts. Then follow the same techniques you used when introducing other signs, keeping in mind that repetition plus consistency equals success.

By the time a baby reaches the stage when they're combining signs, they could be saying a few words too, but usually, the sign combinations come first. Make sure your efforts are now even more focused on their speech development. Use signs as a means of support and motivation.

Signing in Sentences

You might look at signing combinations as baby sentences. When a baby signs DOG and BALL, they're really saying: "The dog has a ball." If they sign EAT and ALL DONE, they're telling you they can't eat another bite. These combinations represent a major stride in the way a baby's thinking. Putting two concepts together is a big deal for any baby. Lavish them with praise and cheer them on!

Don't expect any signing combinations much before 18 months and maybe much later. They almost always happen when a baby should be speaking. That's why many babies use a combination of the two: making a sign and saying a word. However, you might find your baby requests "MORE MILK" or "BOOK AGAIN" before using speech. Be prepared to continue expanding your baby's language use.

Your Little Conversationalist

In Joseph Garcia's book *Sign With Your Baby* (see Appendix E), he talks about a time when one of his sons actually started a conversation by making a sign. According to Garcia, he and his sons had seen a few airplanes the day before and had fun making the sign whenever they saw one. A few days later, while in his high chair, one son started making the AIRPLANE sign. Garcia was puzzled, as there were obviously no airplanes landing in the kitchen. And then it dawned on him. His son was recalling the experience from the day before and simply wanted to talk about it.

Was Garcia's belief based on reality or just wishful thinking? Was the baby actually initiating a conversation or was he just having fun with his hands? Who knows for sure, but because the possibility does exist, why ignore it? If your baby makes a sign out of context, take the cue and start talking about airplanes or whatever else they're signing about.

You might say: "Yes, I remember those airplanes. Weren't they big and beautiful?" Then if you can, find a picture of an airplane to reinforce the idea and sign at the same time. At the very least, these kinds of interactions help stimulate your baby's overall language ability and will bring you closer together.

Some Helpful Reminders

- When you're teaching a sign, use every tool you can think of to help your baby make an association. Voice and body language should be at the top of the list. The look on your face, the tone of your voice, and your general demeanor will help convey vital information.

- Even if you choose not to introduce some signs to your baby, they might still pick them up. For example, don't be surprised if you tell your baby to do something and they look at you and sign "NO!"

- Most parents consider baby sign language as an interim method of communication and teach 10 to 20 signs. How long you sign with your baby and how many signs you teach are up to you. Research shows that even a limited exposure to sign language will benefit your baby.

- Babies love repetition. It not only makes them feel comfortable when they're able to predict outcomes, but it also makes them feel more in control. The problem is that while babies love repetition, adults don't. Try to vary the routines and come up with different ways to help your baby make the necessary associations.

- How quickly you introduce new signs depends on your baby. Introduce one or two and see how fast they catch on. Once your baby figures out that by making gestures their life will get easier, they'll love learning new signs. Even if you give them more than they can initially handle, they'll eventually figure it out.

- Whenever you offer a new word/sign to your baby, it makes another connection within the brain. Words are stored on the left side of the brain and visual information (signs) is stored on the right. The more you speak and sign to your baby, the more their brain is stimulated.

- Don't panic or express disappointment if your baby doesn't sign in a particular situation when they might have signed in that same situation before. They might simply not be in the mood. You don't always feel like talking, do you? Try to motivate them with a happy face and a few signing repetitions. If nothing happens, there's always tomorrow.

Staying the Course

At this stage in the process, you feel one of two ways: You can't wait for your baby to reach the signing stage (if they're not already there) or you're a bit overwhelmed and are having second thoughts about the whole thing. Remember that teaching your baby to sign is just like teaching them to speak—except you're going to include a few visuals (signs) to add emphasis to what you're teaching. This chapter helps you find ways to keep going.

Staying Motivated

What's the number one reason why babies don't sign? Their parents lose their motivation and stop. It does takes patience and commitment to teach sign language to your baby. And it's true you could go months waving your hands in the air without any reaction or feedback from your baby. But it will happen.

All babies have different developmental timetables and will crawl, walk, sign, and talk when they're ready. You'll know if a real concern exists—you'll instinctively reach out to your pediatrician. But not signing yet at a year old is still okay.

If you're really to the point of abandoning your efforts, then consider the express program (Chapter 5). If you've been signing with your baby and started after six months and feel you should be seeing more results than you are, this method is for you.

Motivational Tips and Tactics

Signing can feel a bit repetitive. But keep in mind that babies and toddlers thrive on repetition. Plus, it's only a short-term situation—one that will vanish the moment your baby makes their first sign. When that happens, you won't be able to stop yourself from grabbing your phone or camera to record the moment for posterity. Your enthusiasm will be rekindled and you'll be proud of what you've accomplished—as you should be. Hang in there and keep your eyes on the goal.

But while you're waiting for that day, here are some tips that might help you keep the faith:

- Try focusing on the actual process of communicating with your baby and not just on the outcome. Appreciate the fact you have such a wonderful treasure and be thankful for what they're doing today.

- Re-energize yourself by re-reading Chapter 2 on the benefits for you and your baby.

- Don't think of this as an educational exercise. Think of it as entertainment or as a challenge.

- Ignore other people's comments about why it's not working, what you're doing wrong, or how they were more successful.

- Don't start too early. Start signing when you're likely to get immediate feedback.

- Keep signing in the same situations. Once it gets to be habitual, you might not even realize you're signing until one day, when you least expect it, those little hands will start flying.

- Share your experiences with others. There are online groups for parents at various stages in the signing process (see Appendix E). Some parents have just started or are about to. Others have been at it for months. Join in the experience and ask a question, share your thoughts, brag about your baby, and have a laugh with parents from all over the world. But remember, no two babies are alike, and hard as it might be, use their success stories as inspirations, not as comparisons.

Finding the Time

If one of the reasons you're feeling a bit uneasy has to do with time constraints, perhaps these suggestions will help:

- No one expects you to be a baby sign language expert. You only need to know a few basic signs.

- You can teach as few or as many signs as you want. The number of signs you teach isn't nearly as critical as the quality of the interactions you have with your baby.

- Even if you just teach a few basic signs, your baby will benefit. If you find the time to teach them more, go for it.

- Of course, you shouldn't ignore your older children. Get them involved in this too. They'll love it!

- You don't have to turn your world upside down to be successful. Work signing into your everyday routines. Do what you can. You'll find it's easier than you thought.

What If I Work Outside the Home?

Is it even possible to teach a baby to sign if you spend significant time away from them? The answer: Yes, it's certainly possible. Regardless of how many hours in the day you're away from your baby, you can still give them the gift of signing. You simply need to have a plan:

- Make a list of all the caregivers in your baby's life. Do you have a babysitter? Does a relative watch them? Do you take them to a daycare center or preschool?

Write their names down. Start thinking about how you'll educate and update everyone on that list. Make sure your strategy includes a regular method for them to update you on your child's signing progress and vice versa.

- If your child is about to enter a daycare center or preschool, find one that's signer-friendly. Many incorporate sign language into their curriculum. That's the ideal situation. If not, why not be proactive? More and more daycare centers and childcare facilities are looking for ways to enrich their teachers' training and incorporate new practices to benefit their students. Call on a few and get their reaction. Many parents are likely on the same quest you are. Plus, childcare is a more productive experience for teachers when they have a signing clientele.

- If you're using the express method, getting your daycare or childcare center involved is more important than ever. The express method takes all the elements of teaching sign language and consolidates them into a two-week training session. It's important that everyone who comes into contact with your baby within that framework signs with them in a coordinated effort. Because many daycare centers use signing, this might not be a major problem for you. You can even provide resources. If you can't get the cooperation of your daycare center, just strengthen your own efforts. Sure, it might take longer than two weeks, but it will happen. Just don't get discouraged.

If you can't find a situation that's signer-friendly, try these methods:

- Let your sitter/childcare teacher know from the very beginning that you're signing with your baby.

- Demonstrate the signs your baby's likely to use.

- Bring a sign language book or something similar you can leave for reference.

- Let your caregiver know which signs you're working on and ask them to be on the lookout for them. Ask for a daily progress report.

- Keep the lines of communication open between you and your child's caregiver. Invite questions and promote a dialogue at every opportunity.

When you bring your baby home from daycare, sign as much as you can in whatever situations are natural and appropriate. You can teach your baby to sign even if you're not with your baby 24/7. Will it take longer to see results? Perhaps. But more people signing in more situations could speed things up.

Request Help

Regardless of whether you work in or outside the home, you have another valuable resource you should ask to help with achieving signing success: family. Not only will they make the process easier, but they'll also make the experience much more fun. Remember the old adage about many hands making lighter work. It takes on a literal meaning in this case.

Because your baby will benefit from many role models, recruit as many as you possibly can:

- **Grandparents.** If you're lucky enough to have grandparents nearby, their involvement is critical. Chances are they never signed to you as a baby and might think the idea is a little unusual. This means that before you teach them the signs your baby's making, you might need to promote the concept. Let them borrow this book or sit down with them apart from the rest of the family for a little one-on-one. Hopefully, your enthusiasm will be contagious. They might even get motivated watching you along the way.

- **Big brothers and sisters.** Be sure to include older siblings in this endeavor. They'll love the attention they'll receive and they'll feel special teaching their little brother or sister something of real value. They'll probably pick up signs quickly and can be a wonderful assistant teacher for your baby.

- **Babysitters.** Have sitters arrive early so you can explain what you're doing and the importance of their role in it or so you can give them the rundown of baby's new signs. The "Baby Sign Language Journal" in Appendix F is a great resource for new sitters in interpreting what your baby might be trying to "say." Of course, don't just hand them the journal as you walk out the door. Demonstrate the signs yourself, leaving the journal for reference and reinforcement. Place a copy of the journal on the refrigerator or in some other conspicuous place. By keeping it updated with your baby's progress, all family members and babysitters will know exactly what's going on.

It's a good idea to educate everyone right from the beginning—if at all possible before your baby's ready to start to sign. Encourage everyone to read this book or at the very least have a general understanding of the process, make sure they know what your goals are, and keep them updated on your baby's progress.

If you get new contributors after the mission has begun, bring them up to date right away. Make certain they know the signs your baby's currently making—plus the ones they haven't caught on to yet. You never know who'll be the first one to spot a new sign!

One final piece of advice about getting family members involved: Think of it as a fun family project—something you all can get excited about while doing something important for the newest addition.

Reinforcements

Now all you need to do is stay on track. You have all the tools and knowledge you need and your motivational level is high. Here are some key points you need to remember:

- Speak as you sign.

- Sign only in context.

- Incorporate signs into everyday routines.

- Repeat the signs you've taught.

- Get family and other caregivers involved.

- Add new signs as your baby's ready.

- Use body language and real-life situations to reinforce what you've taught.

- Praise your baby for their efforts.

- Enjoy the experience!

The Advanced Signer

Research has shown that children up to age three benefit from learning sign language to support their overall speech and language development. Plus, at your child's "advanced age," things will go much faster. In this section, you'll learn some valuable new signs that will help your baby (and you) make it through the "terrible twos" as well as invaluable techniques for how to incorporate sign language into potty training. You'll also see what happens when speech enters the picture.

Sign Language for Toddlers

In this chapter, you'll learn that sign language can benefit a toddler more than at any other age. Up to now, it's been a fun and rewarding experience, but when a child is between 18 and 24 months, sign language takes on a new dimension. They'll discover that while signs were useful to them before, now they're really important. Studies have shown that children can benefit from sign language until the age of three—and maybe older—in terms of supporting language acquisition and development. No matter where you and your baby are in their sign language process, you're in the right place.

Why It's a Good Idea

Like many parents, you've heard about the benefits that signing offers. (Read the beginning chapters if you haven't.) In effect, when you sign with a baby or toddler, you stimulate more of their brain and open the door to a host of other developmental extras. Signing helps accelerate language development, builds larger vocabularies, and makes learning to read easier.

On the emotional side, a signing child is less frustrated, has a closer bond with their parents, and feels good about themselves. Studies have shown that one reason for the so-called "terrible twos" is a child's inability to express themselves. Learning to sign can help your child overcome that. Everyone learns differently. Some are visual learners and others are auditory learners. When you teach a toddler to sign, they receive information both ways. This stimulates more of the brain and accelerates learning.

Information Overload

Learning to talk doesn't happen overnight. While toddlers are soaking up information and showing off what they've learned, their language ability is still quite limited and other things get in the way of progress. This is the stage where toddlers are trying out new words, experiencing the power those words have, and beginning to realize there's a whole new world out there. They're experimenting with new words one day, exploring a new part of the house the next day, trying to figure how to climb up the steps the day after that.

While toddlers are trying to become experts at everything, their focus won't always be on communication—until they need to get their point across. Yes, they might be communicating orally to some degree, but the words they need might not always be there. A toddler gets tired or maybe says a word no one can decipher. That can really upset a child. But if a toddler knows a few basic signs and they can use those signs to communicate what they want or what they're feeling, you can see how that can help defuse things—and perhaps prevent a tantrum.

Top 10 Reasons to Sign With a Toddler

- It builds self-confidence and self-esteem.
- It can lead to new friendships if other toddlers use it.
- It gives added emphasis to spoken words.
- It can help overcome shyness.
- It can help express complicated feelings.
- It can help avoid tantrums.
- It's actual language use.
- It can foster bilingualism.
- It helps clarify what they want.
- It continues to develop a deeper bond between parent and child.

Your Job as Translator

Those times when your child won't be able to communicate orally what they want or need are when signs are invaluable to them—and to you as important teaching opportunities. Whenever your toddler makes a sign to get their point across, you should first show you understand what they're trying to communicate. Then you need to take it to the next level and add spoken words. In effect, what you'll do is orally describe what your child is unable to.

For example, if your child is struggling with a wagon in the yard, they might make the sign for HELP. Your job in that moment is to say something like: "What's the matter? Are you trying to pull the wagon and it's stuck? You need HELP? I'll be glad to HELP. Let's pull that wagon together." Of course, while you're saying all that, you're demonstrating the sign. By doing this, you're indicating to your child that you understand their plight and showing them you understand the sign they're making. More importantly, you're also serving as a model for future language development.

Some Advice Before Getting Started

If you've read everything else in this book to this point, you'll have introduced the basic signs to your baby differently from how they're about to be demonstrated. No need to worry: Regardless of what you and your baby have done before, just follow the techniques or adapt them to what you're already doing.

These alternative methods will reinforce what your baby already knows.

Here are a few tips to consider:

- Depending on your toddler's age, what you're about to learn might be more comprehensive than you need at first. Start slowly and move on to another lesson as you see fit.

- Select signing categories that make sense to you and will interest your child.

- Customize the material to the age of your toddler and your own daily routine.

- Teach signs in whatever sequence works best for you and your child.

Your Plan of Action

- If this is your first venture into the world of sign language, decide exactly when you want to begin introducing signs to your toddler. Once you begin, signing needs to be consistent for success.

- Teach the Food and Drink category first because you might find it's the easiest and your child will catch on quickly. Good Manners would be a good next step. You can take it from there.

- Remember that it's not necessary to teach every sign in every category. Use whatever makes sense to you. Select the signs and categories you want your child to learn and memorize them ahead of time. Taking it one category at a time will make it easier.

- Rather than thinking of this as teaching signs, teach associations. Your child might be able to imitate your gestures, but they need to know what they represent before they can use any of them meaningfully.

- Meet with other family members for a practice session. It helps when everyone's familiar with the signs and ready to use them consistently.

- Inform babysitters and teachers about the program and enlist their support. The more people who sign with your child, the better—and the higher the likelihood of success.

- Although you should concentrate on one category for at least a week before moving on to another, you might decide to move on to something different if your child doesn't seem interested. Trust your instincts.

- As with anything else you teach, repetition and reinforcement are key.

- Keep things simple, natural, relaxed, and, by all means, enjoyable.

The toddler stage is a critical moment in a child's life for speech development. Around age one, babies start to talk, but their vocabularies have a long way to go. If they don't have the words at their disposal, signs can help tremendously. In addition, signing places an added emphasis on communication in general—not only for the toddler but for the entire family. This helps explain why children who learn sign language often speak earlier than their nonsigning counterparts. Their parents talk to them more. It's that simple.

What About Talking?

While teaching sign language, you might lose focus on teaching your child to talk. Teaching sign language is an incredible thing, but it's not your finish line. Remember to always say the corresponding word as you sign—and encourage your toddler to do the same.

Chapter

Learning by Example

You've been teaching baby sign language to your child for a couple years now or maybe you bought this book because of the promise that learning sign language might help your toddler with their communication. Remember, it's never too late to teach baby sign language to your child—whether baby or toddler—and this chapter will help you build on the knowledge they already have or develop the skills they need to become better and stronger communicators.

Teaching Categories

This chapter focuses on six main areas:

- Food and Drink
- Good Manners
- Behavior and Safety
- Activities and Games
- Feelings and Emotions
- Animals

The principles and techniques shown here can be adapted to any other category. Illustrations and instructions for all signs in this chapter—and many more—are also in Appendix A.

Food and Drink Signs

When you teach the signs in this category, you'll use a two-step approach. First, you'll teach some generic signs associated with eating: EAT, DRINK, MORE, and ALL DONE/FINISHED. Once your toddler grasps those concepts, you can present specific labels for the foods they want (or don't want) to eat.

Why is the food and drink category a great place to begin teaching your toddler to sign? Because snacks and mealtimes are already part of your everyday routines. That makes them perfect educational opportunities. When you teach these signs, you're simply capitalizing on an already positive experience—one your child usually likes and looks forward to. When your toddler knows a few related signs, they'll have something else to make their snacks and mealtimes even more fun and interesting.

Teaching in context takes on a whole new meaning in the food and drink department. When you teach a certain food sign, the object is obviously there to help make the association. Stock up ahead of time and be prepared when your toddler finally makes the sign.

Tips and Techniques for Teaching Food and Drink Signs

- There's no right or wrong way to teach a sign. Your goal is to develop a natural way for your toddler to associate the sign with the idea you're trying to convey.

- You can teach the signs in the order here or in any way that seems logical. After all, it has to fit in with your routines. It will help, though, if you learn all the signs in this category before you begin.

- Introduce all first-step signs at one meal (EAT, DRINK, MORE, ALL DONE/ FINISHED). Don't expect your child to remember them all right away. While it might seem like a lot at first, think of it as a "signing showcase"—a presentation of the signs you want them to learn.

EAT: Your hand moves back and forth—toward and away—from your mouth as if eating.

DRINK: Pretend you're holding a glass and taking a sip.

Teaching EAT

It helps to have everyone seated around a table where your child can see what's going on. Then demonstrate that it's time to EAT by showing the sign and taking a bite of food. Then ask another family member if they'd like something to EAT. They respond by saying "Yes, I'd like something to EAT." They then demonstrate the sign and get their "reward."

Ask your child the same question: "Would you like to EAT? I'm hungry. I think it's time to EAT." Every time you say the word, make the sign. Then reinforce it by either taking a bite of something or pretending to eat.

Teaching DRINK

Introduce DRINK by saying and signing the word. Then take a drink of something. Have another family member do the same. Ask others if they'd like a DRINK. They should respond by signing and stressing the word. Repeat this a few times.

MORE: Bring the tips of your fingers together a few times, meeting your hands and fingers at your body's midline.

ALL DONE/FINISHED: Both palms face toward you and then turn over and outward.

Teaching MORE

Ask/sign if anyone would like MORE of something. When someone responds by saying and signing that they'd like MORE, make sure they get something. To bring this lesson home to your child, give them one Cheerio and ask/sign if they'd like MORE. Before they can get upset, give them another. Then repeat. This will help them make the association.

Teaching ALL DONE/FINISHED

Decide on which word you'll use (ALL DONE or FINISHED) and stick with it. When your toddler is finished, ask if they're ALL DONE. Do that a few times. Ask others if they're ALL DONE and have them respond by making the sign before handing their empty plate to you.

In between each signing demonstration, just behave naturally. Laugh and talk about other things. Once in a while, when the time feels right, add a signing demonstration, making it fun for everyone.

Once you start using the signs in food and drink, continue doing this. With enough repetition, your family will feel more comfortable with the idea and your toddler will catch on quickly.

BANANA: One hand "peels" a banana, represented by an upright index finger.

JUICE: Make the sign for DRINK and then finger-spell the letter J—a downward hook made with your pinkie. Alternatively, sign the letter J at the corner of your mouth.

When you feel your toddler has a good grasp of those generic concepts, you can move to the next step and teach signs for specific food and drink items. But remember not to abandon the signs you've already taught. Continue to use them whenever appropriate.

Teach specific food and drink signs the same way you did the generic signs. For example, show a BANANA—make the sign and say the word. A day later, try the sign for JUICE. Repeat them often enough and your child will catch on. One day when you least expect it, they'll look at you and make the sign on their own. Make sure you have lots of everything handy so they understand the connection and the purpose of the signs. Introduce the other signs whenever you like. The important thing is to be consistent.

Good Manners Signs

This category is the perfect step after food and drink signs. Regardless of whether they're spoken or signed, these concepts are difficult for a child to understand. We say PLEASE as part of a request for something and THANK YOU when we get what we asked for. Then the person who gave us whatever we requested responds by saying YOU'RE WELCOME. Will this personally benefit your toddler? Maybe not at the moment. Just think of it as an early introduction to the rules of proper etiquette. Because these signs have no concrete associations for your child to make, focus on repetition to build habit.

Teaching PLEASE, THANK YOU, and YOU'RE WELCOME

The best way to teach the signs for PLEASE and THANK YOU is by example. While your child is at the dinner table with you, ask another family member for something—but use *lots* more spoken emphasis than you would normally. Then exaggerate the sign itself. For example, say to someone "May I PLEASE have a napkin?" When you receive what you asked for, exaggerate THANK YOU as you sign and smile. In return, the person who gave you the napkin must say and sign YOU'RE WELCOME.

Continue this strategy for a few days before you have your child try it themselves. Encourage them by gently taking their hand and guiding it through the signing motion if they're open to the prompt. Only do this occasionally as a way to motivate them—but *never* force them to sign.

Results will depend on the age of your toddler and how often and consistently you sign with them. They might pick up the idea immediately or it could take a few weeks. Stick with it, though, and remember to exaggerate your efforts.

Incorporate the signs into other parts of your daily routines. Whenever you say PLEASE or THANK YOU, make the sign. Add YOU'RE WELCOME whenever appropriate. Remember that your child needs to see other signing situations and applications to fully grasp how good manners signs should be used and in what circumstances.

PLEASE: Your open hand makes a small circle over your chest.

THANK YOU: Your fingertips touch your mouth or chin and then move away from your body.

YOU'RE WELCOME: Your flat open hand moves outward from the front of your face to your waist.

SORRY: Your closed hand makes a small circle over your chest.

Teaching SORRY

SORRY is another sign you can use throughout the day. Introduce this sign when a logical opportunity occurs. Reinforce the SORRY sign with a long face and downturned mouth to communicate your sorrow. And as always, exaggerate your expressions.

You can also use SORRY when managing your child's behavior. Remind them to tell others that they're SORRY about certain actions or behaviors and encourage them to use the sign. Remember to encourage your child to use signs, but don't demand them.

Behavior and Safety Signs

This category has as many positive benefits for your child as it does for you. It gives them a sense of control over their relationships with others, promotes a sense of self, and helps them grow as an individual.

Instead of pushing, pulling, and crying, your child can simply say or sign SHARE. Instead of letting themselves be bullied, a child can just sign STOP. While this might not totally solve the problem (especially if the bully doesn't understand sign language), your little signer will feel more empowered and their overall body language will help convey their meaning.

Use these signs as a way to reinforce positive behavior and to provide safety instructions. A physical gesture makes it more interesting, drawing and keeping attention.

Tips and Techniques for Teaching These Signs

- Because your child often needs to make a personal connection (or association) to learn a sign, wait for a situation when something negative occurs. Then deal one-on-one with the situation, using your tone of voice, facial expression, and body language to help convey your message— along with the sign.

- The manner in which you model each sign will help get your meaning across. For example, STOP should be made clearly, decisively, and emphatically— and then repeated if necessary. It's the same thing with NO.

- Remember to offer spoken praise to your toddler and to reinforce your approval with a sign: GOOD job!

- Consider the following scenario: Let's say you're outdoors and you see your little one on the other side of the playground. You see they're pushing their way toward the front of the line to go down the slide. You can walk over there yourself, pull them out of the line, and admonish them in front of all the other children on the playground. Or you can simply call their name, and with a disapproving look on your face, sign STOP or NO.

SHARE: One hand is held vertically with the thumb up. The other vertical hand slides back and forth over the index finger to convey slicing or dividing something.

STOP: Your flat hand is held vertically and drops forcefully on the palm of your other hand.

NO: Your index and middle fingers snap to your thumb.

GOOD: Your fingertips touch your lips and move slightly away from your mouth.

- Introduce the other signs when it seems logical—when your child can make a connection to the sign. Because signs need to be taught in context, wait for a relevant situation. In other words, wait for a situation when you would naturally say the word and then add its sign.

While the rationale behind most other signs is obvious, two need some extra information to help you use them:

- GENTLE TOUCH. This is a good sign to teach when a friend brings their infant to visit. Just as you use a stern voice for STOP, now your tone becomes calm and soothing. It's also a good sign to use with a new pet in the family. Many children like to grab or squeeze pets and need to be encouraged to take a more gentle approach.

GENTLE TOUCH: One hand gently "pets" the back of the other hand.

- DON'T TOUCH. This is a combination of NO and TOUCH. It might become one of your most popular signs.

Activities and Games Signs

By the time your child is a toddler, you really don't have to worry about bombarding them with too much information—or too many signs. Children's brains have an amazing ability to take in an incredible amount of information and sort it all out. It's like teaching words. You say a certain word over and over, emphasizing it as much as possible. When a child is ready and able to repeat it back to you, they will.

Tips and Techniques for Teaching These Signs

- The signs in this category will serve as an additional method and motivation for your child to express themselves while adding to their signing vocabulary. Because many of these signs look like what they represent (iconic), they'll be easy for your child and you to remember.

- A brief demonstration is all you need for obvious signs. The first time you read a book, show the sign for BOOK. "See how I can make my hands open like a BOOK? That's the way we make the sign!"

- The same goes for BALL. "I'm going to make a sign and I bet you can guess what I'm signing. Yes, it's a BALL! Can you try?"

DON'T TOUCH: A combination of NO and TOUCH. The index and middle fingers snap to the thumb, indicating NO. Then the middle finger of the same hand taps the back of the other hand, indicating TOUCH.

BOOK: Your palms open and close as if opening and closing a book.

- Promote the use of signs by asking your child to choose. "Do you want to play BALL or read a BOOK? Can you speak and sign your choice?"

- Introduce MUSIC and DANCE together for their obvious correlation.

- Sign PLAY and RUN/CHASE ME as part of your routine. Maintain a signing dialogue. "Would you like to PLAY? Let's see how fast you can RUN/CHASE ME."

- Use books to teach the signs. Point to a picture, say the word, and demonstrate the sign. Ask your child to do the same.

- When it's appropriate for you to use a word and you know the sign, go for it.

BALL: Your hands are open as if you're about to catch a ball, showing its round shape.

MUSIC: Your flat hand moves rhythmically back and forth over your opposite arm.

DANCE: Your index and middle fingers swing back and forth over the palm of the other hand, like legs on a dance floor.

PLAY: The thumbs and pinkie fingers of both hands are extended and shake back and forth.

RUN/CHASE: Each hand forms a loose L shape. The index finger of one hand pulls on the thumb of the other. As both hands move forward, the index finger wiggles.

Feelings and Emotions Signs

The benefits of encouraging your toddler to express their emotions by using words and related signs are obvious. Doing this validates their right to feel the way they're feeling. Plus, it gives them a way to let people know exactly how they feel, especially if they're not able to articulate it. Simply put, signing reduces the alternatives: whining, crying, and kicking—to name just a few.

Tips and Techniques for Teaching These Signs

- As you're likely already doing, continue to let your toddler know that having a certain feeling or reaction is fine, but expressing that emotion by talking about it—and signing it—is even better.

- Use books where characters convey specific emotions. Ask questions that promote a discussion of emotions and their related signs. "How do you think the three bears felt when they saw that Goldilocks ate their porridge? Do you think they were ANGRY? Have you ever been ANGRY?"

- Consider creative role-playing to promote the use and understanding of different emotions and signs. Use body language and exaggerated facial expressions to better communicate the meaning of the signs.

ANGRY: Your fingers bend while pulling away from your face.

HURT/PAIN: The tips of your index fingers touch anywhere on your body that feels pain.

- HURT/PAIN isn't exactly an emotional state, but it can result in crying or emotional upheaval. HURT/PAIN is an important sign to know and teach. Because it's a bit more complex than some of the other signs, newcomers to the program should read Chapter 4 for more about how to introduce and reinforce this sign.

Animal Signs

Sometimes while promoting the use of signing to toddlers, we lose sight of the fact it can be just plain fun! No, it isn't necessary for your child to know the animal signs, but they'll enjoy learning them—and you will too.

Tips and Techniques for Teaching These Signs

- Introduce the signs for the various animals in a lesson devoted to the topic.

- Model the sign for each animal using an animal picture book. Your child's favorite storybooks might be the perfect place to start because many include animals.

- Reinforce the sign and the name of the animal by asking your child to sign and make the noise the animal makes.

- Have your toddler make the sign and have others guess what the animal is.

- Take your child to the zoo to reinforce and verify what they've learned.

- It doesn't matter what or how many animal signs you teach. Teach them just for the joy of it.

One of the best ways to reinforce signs is to make them interactive experiences for your child. For example, when teaching your child animal signs, a trip to the zoo takes on a whole new dimension. Not only will they see their picture-book animals come alive, but they'll have something to talk and sign about for days.

Potty Training and Sign Language

I'm not an expert on how to potty train children. My expertise is in helping parents and children communicate through sign language. But because one of the key elements of potty-training readiness and success is a child's ability to communicate their need to use the toilet, bringing the two together is as natural as the process itself. This chapter delves into this delicate but important aspect to raising a child and how sign language can help.

How Sign Language Helps With Potty Training

Numerous programs, philosophies, and theories as to the best way to potty train a child exist. Because it's not my mission to comment on the pros and cons of the different techniques or endorse one idea over another, I'll instead refer you to the many resources available on the topic—some of which are listed in Appendix E. No matter what method you employ, sign language will make it easier, faster, and less stressful on everyone involved. Here's how:

- It makes your toddler feel like they have more control in the process. The toddler stage of development is a time when children begin to realize they don't always have to do what you say. Using signs together helps promote a partnership rather than an adversarial relationship.

- It helps reinforce the potty-training routine. You know how toddlers love having you read the same book over and over? It helps them feel in control when they know what the outcomes are. They also like regularities in their daily routine and it's comforting to be able to predict what comes next. Because sign language in potty training consists of the same signs repeatedly, it reinforces the specific behaviors you're trying to teach.

- It alleviates some of the monotony. We all agree that potty training isn't something we look forward to. In fact, it's probably something you want to get over with as fast as you can. But when you think about it, it's probably not that much fun for a child either. If you vary the experience by signing while reading a book or singing a signing song, it could make the experience more enjoyable—for everyone.

- It eliminates some of the guesswork. Maybe your child isn't speaking yet, but it makes life easier if they can alert you that they have to use the bathroom. If a child can sign, there might be fewer accidents. That alone is worth the effort.

Getting an Earlier Start

Using sign language in conjunction with potty training can help you start earlier with training. According to *Baby Signs* creators and baby sign language pioneers Drs. Susan Goodwyn and Linda Acredolo, whom you met in Chapter 1, potty training has gotten older over the years. In their book *A Parent's Guide to Potty Training*, they say the main culprit is the disposable diaper. With disposables being available as large as size 6T, parents can wait longer, and because these diapers do a remarkable job of keeping the little ones dry and comfortable, most toddlers don't seem to mind one little bit. Many might even enjoy the one-on-one personal valet service.

The other reason for the trend toward later potty training is that many pediatricians say to wait until toddlers decide to start on their own. Many parents take that advice and simply wait it out, leading to challenges with success.

It's About Being Ready

While Acredolo and Goodwyn recommend potty training before age two, many experts say to wait until a child is developmentally ready—with one of the primary benchmarks being whether they can communicate their need to use the toilet. Even if a child isn't saying a single word, sign language makes that communication possible. Goodwyn and Acredolo suggest it can happen before age two.

The Readiness Checklist

"Readiness" means cognitive and physical readiness as far as the potty-training process itself. You already know your child is ready and able to use signs—even if you haven't taught them any yet. But let's see if they're ready in other areas:

- They stay dry for longer periods of time—for two hours or more—which indicates increasing bladder capacity.

- They recognize when they're in the process of urinating or voiding.

- They're able to easily pull their training pants up and down.

- They can follow simple instructions.

- They're able to sit and focus on an activity for several minutes without becoming distracted or irritable.

- They show interest, desire, and/or curiosity about the potty.

POTTY/TOILET: Your index finger folds over your thumb (in a T shape). With the thumb peeking out, shake your fist back and forth.

Beginning the Process

Now that you're convinced the idea of signing in this situation is a good idea, it's time to incorporate signs. You really don't need a lot of additional instruction to figure out how to introduce signs in potty training. Simply sign and say "POTTY. Time to go POTTY" and then add additional signs at the appropriate stages. Continue to reinforce the potty and signing routine repeatedly to make this a habit.

The potty-training signs reflect the sequence:

- POTTY/TOILET
- PAPER
- ALL DONE/FINISHED
- WASH HANDS
- GOOD

PAPER: The heel of one palm brushes against the other and toward your body.

ALL DONE/FINISHED: Both palms face toward you and then turn over and outward.

WASH HANDS: The fingers of one hand make a circle in the palm of the other to represent rubbing soap in the hand.

GOOD: Your fingertips touch your lips and move slightly away from your mouth. (This can also be used for GOOD JOB.)

You can also use these other signs to vary the routine or introduce other factors involved when necessary. Use them to create and reinforce an awareness of the entire process:

- DRY
- HURRY
- DIAPER CHANGE

HURRY: The index and middle fingers on both hands (in an H shape) are extended and rapidly move forward in an up-and-down motion.

DRY: The index finger wipes across the chin or upper lip as if drying it.

DIAPER CHANGE: All fingers except your thumb fold to your palms. Bring your knuckles together and pivot in opposite directions with both hands.

Tips and Techniques

Three steps are usually involved when teaching your child anything:

1. Present your learning objectives.

2. Reinforce those objectives.

3. Reward success.

While signs can help you reinforce each step, this isn't an exact science with a guaranteed recipe for success. Rather than a step-by-step approach, here are some suggestions and guidelines you can follow:

- Start introducing all signs now. Many are applicable in any number of situations in addition to the bathroom. For example, ALL DONE, WASH HANDS, and GOOD could work as well at mealtime as they do at bathroom time. If you haven't already done this, start introducing the signs into your everyday routines.

- If you've taught the sign for DIAPER CHANGE, continue to use it. It will help create an awareness of the process—and bring enhanced awareness of the diaper when it's wet, dry, on, and off.

- Pick a starting date and stick to it. Once you start to introduce signs at bathroom time, it's essential you reinforce them.

- Once the child is on the potty, establish a sequence and stick to that. It's critical you maintain the same routine every time. Your child will come to expect to see the signs and hear the words that go with them. They'll begin to realize what behaviors are expected with each sign.

BOOK: *Your palms open and close as if opening and closing a book.*

HELP: *Your open palms tap your chest twice.*

- Once your child knows the sequence, you can introduce some ancillary signs as needed, such as HELP or BOOK. (Sitting on the potty with a book is often a good idea and helps prevent boredom.)

- Keep an eye on your child to establish their bathroom routines and use them to help you predict when your child needs to use the potty. For example, when you get them out of the crib after a nap, say right away: "It's time to use the POTTY!" Then make the sign. Don't ask if they have to use the potty—just establish the routine without making it optional.

- When your child has experienced any level of success, be sure to praise them by the look on your face, with words, and, of course, the sign for GOOD!

The Reward System

The last step warrants additional attention. It's imperative to recognize your child for a job well done. There are many ways to do this and each depends on what your child responds to best. You don't need to do anything particular, but you do need techniques to motivate your child and reward their accomplishments. For some children, just your voice along with the big smile on your face will be enough of a motivator for them to continue. But other children respond better with visual reinforcement. A simple chart on the wall with smiley stickers on successful days can go a long way toward helping you reach your—and their—goal.

Look Who Can Talk!

By now, you've found teaching your baby to sign to be a memorable experience. You can still continue the process and keep teaching new signs, but even if you don't, they'll still use the ones they know for quite some time. This chapter will help you shift from teaching sign language to supporting your child with their developing speech skills.

Keep on Signing

When your baby starts to say a few words, don't stop signing to them. In fact, encouraging them to sign will help them make the transition to spoken language easier.

According to *Baby Signs* researchers Linda Acredolo and Susan Goodwyn, babies can benefit from sign language until they're two and a half years old. Other researchers say up to age three. They're still within that window of opportunity when their brains are primed for maximum stimulation in the language department. The longer you speak and sign with your baby, the brainier they'll become.

Think about that for a minute: If your baby said their first word at 12 months, their brain will be positively impacted by sign language for another 18 months. And their brain will be *permanently* impacted by that throughout their entire life!

Why is that? Spoken information (your voice) is received and stored on the brain's left side. Visual information (signs) is received and stored on the right side. Because sign language involves audio and video, more of the brain is stimulated. When your baby needs to search and recall information, they have two sources to tap into. The result? A smarter baby with a larger vocabulary who'll also have an easier time learning to read. And that doesn't even begin to address the *emotional* benefits.

Continue to reinforce the signs that your baby already knows and introduce new words and signs when opportunities present themselves. In other words, just keep doing what you've been doing.

Why They'll Speak Rather Than Sign

What will happen if you stop signing with your baby once they start to speak? They'll eventually drop their signs in favor of spoken words. Yes, they'll have enjoyed the experience and benefitted in so many ways, but in a hearing family, their ultimate goal is speech.

Why would a baby use sign language when they can speak? One reason might be for emphasis—to make sure they're really getting their point across. For example, they might use DON'T TOUCH when you want to change their diaper or NO when you tell them it's time to go to bed.

Like everything else, their developing speech happens in stages. When your baby reaches a certain level in their development, they'll want to do what you're doing—which is speaking.

How It Will All Play Out

While your baby might begin to use speech more regularly, their signs won't disappear overnight. Most babies use them well after they've begun to talk and will keep them as long as they're useful. That's important to remember. As long as a sign helps your baby or holds some interest for them, they'll continue to use it. But that also means that while you might continue to reinforce their old signs or try to teach them new ones, if it's not your primary language and the signs aren't relevant or meaningful to them, you might be wasting your time.

Why would a sign be useful for a baby when they're learning to talk? Maybe the word they want to articulate is multisyllabic. Try saying that sentence when you're 13 months old! Or perhaps they're just tired and they don't want to bother. Think of the reasons you use sign language. You don't sign? Maybe you don't use ASL, but you do gesture:

- You use signs and gestures for emphasis. "STOP right there and take off those muddy boots before you come in the house." It's more effective when you hold your palm out in front of you, isn't it?

- What about when words just won't cut it? "I swear, the fish I caught was this BIG."

- When you're doing something and your child diverts your attention by asking where something is. If you know where it is, you point to it. If you don't, you shrug your shoulders.

- When you spot a friend across a crowded room and want them to TELEPHONE you later. Thumb to your ear and pinkie to your mouth. (That *is* an ASL sign.)

Your baby will continue to use signs for those very same reasons: for emphasis, clarification, and maybe out of habit—at least for a while. When will they stop? It's hard to say. As before, too many variables exist.

Regardless of when the transition to speech does occur, it almost always happens in stages. Of course, there are exceptions. There always are when it comes to a baby's growth and development. But generally speaking, here's what you can expect:

- Your baby will sign on their own without any prompting.

- They'll say (or attempt to say) the word along with the sign.

- They'll drop most signs and keep a few favorites for clarification or emphasis.

- Words will take over and they'll drop the signs altogether.

You should be aware that at some point during the transition, your baby might have two separate vocabularies—one of signs and another of words. They might devote all their energy to building their speaking vocabulary and not be interested in learning any new signs. They might be perfectly happy with the ones they already know. If you'd like them to learn a few more, try again in a few weeks.

On the other hand, they might be the type who just can't get enough. They want to have it all. If that's the case, they might be open to learning new words and new signs. You just can't predict. Follow the leader.

Taking Corrective Action

Making the move from signing to speech is a complicated process for your baby. In effect, they're trading in one set of symbols (signs) for another one (words). Give them room to experiment with what works and what doesn't. But be vigilant! The signs they're making might be clues to what they're trying to say. They might help you decipher their meaning.

BOTTLE: Pretend to grip a bottle with one hand and place it on the palm of your other hand.

At first, you should expect that your baby's signs will be more accurate than their words. After all, they've been signing much longer than they've been talking. Pay close attention to their signs and body language. When you can figure out what your baby's saying, it's less frustrating for everyone involved.

Here's another important tip: Do you recall when your baby was beginning to sign and wasn't able to make the signs accurately at first? But you applauded their attempts anyway, right? Then you reinforced each effort by saying the word and showing them the correct way to make the sign.

Do the same thing now. For example, if your baby says "Bah" for bottle, show them how pleased you are that they're trying to speak. Maybe they've also made the sign for BOTTLE along with "Bah" so you know for sure what they're trying to tell you.

Let them know you understand by making the sign for BOTTLE. Then say something like: "BOTTLE! Yes, of course you can have your BOTTLE." Make sure you carefully model the word as it's actually said—the way you model signs rather than repeating your child's approximations.

You and Your Baby's Secret Signs

There's another reason why you and your baby might want to hold on to some signs, even well beyond the stage when they have the ability to use speech. Some signs might be or can become personal ways to communicate with one another without letting the rest of the world in on it—at least the ones who don't sign anyway. For example, DON'T TOUCH is a sign you and your baby could use even when they get a bit older.

Another suggestion is the sign for POTTY/TOILET. When your take your toddler to the park, they might lose track of time and not think about going to the restroom until it's too late. Instead of embarrassing them in front of their friends, occasionally flash the sign with an inquisitive look to ask them to think about using the facilities.

HELP can also come in handy when speaking isn't an option or you don't want to call attention to something.

These are just a few situations when it might pay to be silent. You'll discover some of your own—including and hopefully especially the sign for I LOVE YOU.

DON'T TOUCH: *The index and middle fingers snap to the thumb, indicating NO. Then the middle finger of the same hand taps the back of the other hand, indicating TOUCH.*

HELP: *Your open palms tap your chest twice.*

POTTY/TOILET: *Your index finger folds over your thumb (in a T shape). With the thumb peeking out, shake your fist back and forth.*

I LOVE YOU: *Extend your pinkie, index finger, and thumb.*

Dealing With Speech and Language Development Concerns

While there might be any number of reasons why children have challenges speaking, none are caused by their having learned sign language as babies. In fact, a growing number of speech pathologists are using signs to augment traditional therapy and stimulate spoken language development in older children. But this is still a concern parents might have.

Just to make sure we're on the same page, let's start with some definitions. Exactly what is language and how is it defined? Simply put, language is the way we communicate with one another. It's a system of sounds and symbols we use to express meanings, ideas, thoughts, and our inner feelings. To communicate with one another, everyone needs to know the symbols and the rules on how these symbols go together (known as "syntax").

Speech is part of language. It's a mechanical process that results in the formation of sounds and words. But speech is only one way language is expressed. Writing and signing are others.

To help you understand the difference, consider a situation in which a speech pathologist in the public school system has a large caseload of students—some of whom are being seen for language disorders and others for speech disorders. Some language students have problems fully understanding what was said to them. Others have difficulty expressing themselves to others. Their speech was absolutely fine. It was processing the information that was giving them trouble.

Students with speech problems had difficulty with the mechanics of producing particular sounds. Problems ranged in severity from a simple substitution problem ("wabbit" instead of "rabbit") to children who made so many substitutions and sound additions that their speech was almost impossible to understand.

What's a parent to do if you think there's a problem? If you think your child isn't speaking when they should or not as much as they should or if others have a hard time understanding them, consult the following timeline. Keep in mind that because children speak and learn language at different rates, the timetable is broad. That means that if your child's behaviors don't match others of the same age, there might be no need to panic.

Speech and Language Development Timeline

Age	Activity
Birth to 3 months	• Makes pleasure sounds (cooing) • Cries differently for different needs
3 to 6 months	• Increased interest in sounds and voices • Responds to changes in your voice • Makes gurgling sounds • Babbling sounds more like speech and includes different sounds, including *p*, *b*, and *m*
6 to 9 months	• Turns and looks in the direction of sounds • Understands that vocalizations get attention • Understands their first words • Can imitate gestures and manipulate objects
9 to 12 months	• Begins to understand simple instructions, such as "Wave bye-bye" • Understands approximately 12 words by 12 months (names of family members, pets, body parts, basic clothing, etc.) • Might say their first word. Most babies speak their first words between 10 and 15 months. The average is 12 months. • Recognizes words for common items, such as cup, shoe, and juice • Begins to respond to requests, such as "Come here." and "Want more?" • Uses speech and noncrying sounds to get and keep attention • Imitates different speech sounds • Has one or two spoken words ("bye-bye," "dada," "mama"), although they might not be clear

Speech and Language Development Timeline (continued)

Age	Activity
12 to 24 months	• Receptive vocabulary increases to as many as 300 words • Spoken language increases to an average of 200 to 275 words • Points to body parts when asked • Follows simple commands • Points to pictures in books • Says more words every month • Asks two-word questions ("Go bye-bye?") • Puts two words together ("more juice")
24 to 36 months	• Vocabulary continues to grow • Asks "why" questions • Uses "no" and "not" • Enjoys naming objects in picture books

Source: *US Department of Education*

The Late-Talker Quiz

1. Does your 18-month-old say any words clearly?

2. Does your 20-month-old follow simple requests, such as "Come to Daddy"?

3. Does your 24-month-old put two words together, such as "more juice"?

4. Does your 2-year-old ask questions and respond to simple questions with "Yes" or "No"?

5. Does your 3- or 4-year-old use language freely, experiment with oral sounds, and begin to use language to solve problems and learn concepts?

6. Do most people outside your family and other caregivers understand what your 3-year-old is saying?

Now ask yourself this final question: Do your instincts tell you something's wrong? If the answer to this last question is "Yes" and you answered "No" to any of the questions, then it's time to take the next step.

What to Do and When to Do It

We don't often know the reason why a child is a late-talker. Rather than worry about what caused it, take action and get professional help to correct it. Talk to a pediatrician. Chances are, the doctor will refer you to a speech and language pathologist (SLP), who'll evaluate your child with special tests. A hearing test will also be included to rule out the possibility of related hearing loss.

Based on the test results, the SLP might suggest activities to do at home to stimulate development in this area. Often, that's all it takes. You might be advised to read more, use simpler words, and speak in shorter sentences to make imitation easier. You might also be encouraged to repeat what your child says, using correct grammar and pronunciation. This would enable you to demonstrate more accurate speech and language behaviors without directly correcting them. There are many different ways to tackle the problem.

It's critical that an SLP make the determination about teaching sign language to children with delayed speech. Don't assume that sign language will help your late-talking child and take it upon yourself to start. Without professional guidance, your child might learn there's little or no need to speak when sign language works just fine, complicating the situation even further.

Sometimes, the SLP will look at the tests, the age of your child, and the extent of the delay and then recommend group or individual therapy. If your child is having difficulty being understood, the pathologist might also recommend sign language to reduce the frustration that can result.

It's important to remember that some children are just slow speakers and simply need a bit more prompting. Sign language might help as an interim way for them to express themselves while stimulating their spoken language. If used properly, these late-talkers might speak sooner than they otherwise might have.

Sign Language and Children With Special Needs

This book is meant to help pre-verbal hearing babies communicate with their parents through sign language. While sign language is a wonderful gift to give a child, a hearing baby will eventually learn to communicate without it. In other words, parents of hearing babies use sign language to enhance communication, not establish it. If you're the parent of a Deaf baby, you'll want to use a more comprehensive and serious method of addressing the special needs of your child.

In addition to the Deaf and hard of hearing, other children with special needs might benefit from using sign language. Teachers and parents of children with Down syndrome have credited sign language with making a huge difference in their children's communication skills as well as reducing their frustration with being understood.

Like all other kids, children with Down syndrome develop at different rates, but in general, all learn and develop more slowly than the norm. Low muscle tone and difficulty with tongue mobility affect speech production and can make speech difficult to understand. Add to that the fact that most children with Down syndrome have trouble recalling and organizing information and you can understand the major communication problems that can result.

Recent studies in this area appear to offer a new direction. Basically, they say that while children with Down syndrome tend to have difficulties with auditory learning, using sign language capitalizes on their visual strengths, helping them gain confidence and become less frustrated as well as paving the way for learning speech at their own pace.

Children with other learning challenges might also benefit from sign language:

- Children with autism might find it useful as a way to communicate.

- Because of related brain trauma impacting speech development, some children with cerebral palsy find that sign language facilitates communication.

- Children with attention deficit hyperactivity disorder (ADHD) can benefit from the use of sign language. Using their hands to communicate occupies their minds and gives them the ability to stay on task. That helps develop impulse control and self-confidence.

Is sign language the ultimate solution or a panacea for children with special needs? Not necessarily, but it can be an effective tool and source of support. Parents and therapists who use sign language with children who have special needs say it sure beats pointing and grunting. Because sign language is something most children can learn easily, it also promotes positive situations that stimulate greater learning and often improved speech and language skills. Plus, sign language has the ability to decrease challenging behaviors that might result when a child has trouble expressing themselves.

Baby Sign Language Dictionary

Beginning Signs

Beginning signs are listed here in their order of importance according to research.
Consider introducing them to your baby in this sequence.

more

more

Bring your fingertips together a few times,
meeting your hands at your body's midline.

eat

eat

Your hand moves back and forth—toward
and away—from your mouth as if eating.

milk

milk

Your hand opens and closes as if you're milking a cow.

hurt/pain

hurt/pain

The tips of your index fingers touch anywhere on your body that feels pain.

help #1

help

Your open palms tap your chest twice.

help #2

help #2

One hand lifts the other hand to represent the concept of "assistance."

diaper change

diaper change

All fingers except your thumb fold to your palms. Bring your knuckles together and pivot in opposite directions with both hands. (This is the sign for CHANGE, with DIAPER being implied.)

Food and Drink

The signs for EAT, MILK, and MORE are under "Beginning Signs." ALL DONE/FINISHED is under "Potty Training."

apple

The knuckle of your index finger touches your cheek while your closed hand twists forward.

apple

banana

One hand "peels" a banana, represented by the upright index finger on the other hand.

banana

bottle

Pretend to grip a bottle with one hand and place it on the palm of your other hand.

bottle

breastfeed

Your flat palm lightly brushes the breast in a downward motion.

breastfeed

cookie

cookie

Your fingers in a "C" shape make a circular motion on the opposite palm as if using a cookie cutter on dough.

cracker

cracker

Tap a closed hand against the opposite elbow.

drink

drink

Pretend you're holding a glass and taking a sip.

ice cream

ice cream

Position your hand as if you were holding and licking an ice cream cone.

juice

Make the sign for drink and then fingerspell the letter J—a downward hook made with your pinkie. Alternatively, sign the letter J at the corner of your mouth.

juice

orange

One hand mimics squeezing an orange in front of your mouth.

orange

water

water

Make a W with three fingers and tap your lips with the index finger of the W.

Good Manners

please

please

Your open hand makes a small circle over your chest.

sorry

sorry

Your closed hand makes a small circle over your chest.

thank you

Your fingertips touch your mouth or chin and then move away from your body.

thank you

you're welcome

Your flat open hand moves outward from the front of your face to your waist.

you're welcome

Feelings and Emotions

The sign for SORRY is under "Good Manners."

angry

Your fingers bend while pulling away from your face.

angry

cold

Your shoulders are hunched forward. Your hands shake as if they're cold.

cold

cry

cry

The index fingers of both hands alternately trace tears rolling down your cheeks.

frightened

frightened

Your hands move in front of your body as if you're trying to protect yourself. Change your fingers from closed to splayed.

happy

Your hand moves upward on your chest, indicating "high spirits."

happy

hot

Your hand in a C shape moves to your mouth as if you're about to eat, but then the hand turns and moves away quickly as if the food's too hot.

hot

hug

hug

Cross both arms over your chest and grip the opposite arm as if you're hugging yourself.

I love you

I love you

Extend your pinkie, index finger, and thumb.

love

love

Cross your closed fists over your heart.

sad

sad

The fingers of both hands are outspread and move down your face from your eyebrows to your mouth.

Behavior and Safety

The sign for HELP is under "Beginning Signs." The sign for WHERE is under "Independence."

bed

bed

Rest your tilted head on your hands.

bed

clean

clean

One hand wipes "dirt" off the other one multiple times, with your palms facing.

clean

don't touch

don't touch

A combination of NO and TOUCH. The index and middle fingers snap to the thumb, indicating NO. Then the middle finger of that hand taps the back of the other hand, indicating TOUCH.

gentle touch

gentle touch

One hand gently "pets" the back of the other.

good

Your fingertips touch your lips and move slightly away from your mouth. (This can also be used for GOOD JOB.)

good

listen

Cup your hand to your ear.

listen

no

no

The index and middle fingers snap to the thumb.

quiet

quiet

The index fingers start at the mouth with one hand in front of the other. Then they move downward in a silencing gesture.

share

One hand is held vertically with the thumb up. The other vertical hand slides back and forth over the index finger to convey slicing or dividing something.

share

sit

The first two fingers of one hand "sit" on the same two fingers of the other hand.

sit

sleep

sleep

Your hand is held in front of your face. Your fingers are then drawn to your mouth and close as if they're eyelids shutting.

slow

slow

With both palms facing down, one hand moves slowly up the back of the other from fingertips to forearm.

speak

Your index fingers alternately move back and forth from your mouth.

speak

stop

Your flat hand is held vertically and drops forcefully on the palm of your other hand.

stop

wait

Your palms are held upward and your fingers wiggle. One hand is slightly in front of the other.

wait

yes

Your closed fist moves up and down.

yes

Activities and Games

ball

ball

Your hands are open as if you're about to catch a ball, showing its round shape.

book

book

Your palms open and close as if opening and closing a book.

computer

Your hand is shaped like a C and moves along your forearm.

computer

dance

Your index and middle fingers swing back and forth over the palm of the other hand, like legs on a dance floor.

dance

fall

Your fingers make a V and stand on your palm, then lie flat to indicate falling.

fall

hide

One closed fist with your thumb pointing up "hides" beneath the opposite cupped palm.

hide

jump

Your fingers form a downward V and they jump up and down from your open palm, bending at the knuckles.

jump

music

Your flat hand moves rhythmically back and forth over your opposite arm.

music

paint

The movement of the fingers represents a paintbrush applying paint to a surface.

paint

play

The thumbs and pinkie fingers of both hands are extended and shake back and forth.

play

run/chase

run

Each hand forms a loose L shape. The index finger of one hand pulls on the thumb of the other. As both hands move forward, the index finger wiggles.

swim

swim

Your hands and arms mimic a swimmer's actions.

swing

Your index and middle fingers grab the same two fingers of the other hand and swing forward.

swing

telephone

Your thumb is at your ear and your pinkie is at your mouth.

telephone

walk

walk

Your flat hands represent feet. The movement of the fingers "stepping" represents walking.

Clothing

coat

Mime putting on a coat by pulling it forward from your shoulders.

coat

hat

Your open hand pats the top of your head.

hat

pants

The movement of the hands indicates the legs on a pair of pants. Open palms slide down both legs.

pants

shirt

With your index finger and thumb, grab your shirt in the upper chest area and tug outward a few times.

shirt

shoes

shoes

Tap your two downward fists together twice.

socks

socks

Both index fingers point down. One moves up and the other down, brushing against each other.

Family

mommy

mommy

The thumb of your open hand taps your chin twice.

daddy

daddy

The thumb of your open hand taps your forehead twice.

grandmother

The thumb of your open hand starts at your wchin and then makes two arcs down and away.

grandmother

grandfather

The thumb of your open hand starts at your forehead and then makes two arcs down and away.

grandfather

sister

One hand forms an L with the thumb touching the chin. It then moves downward to meet the other L-shaped hand.

sister

brother

One hand forms an L with the thumb touching the forehead. It then moves downward to meet the other L-shaped hand.

brother

baby

baby

One arm cradles the other and both move side to side in a rocking motion.

Independence

The sign for HELP is under "Beginning Signs." The sign for STOP is under "Behavior and Safety."

down

down

Your index finger points downward.

mine

mine

Bring your open palm toward your chest to signify ownership.

up

Your index finger points upward.

up

want

Both hands are extended and then brought toward the body while the fingers curl up as if pulling open a drawer.

want

where

where

Wag your index finger from side to side.

yours

yours

An open hand moves toward the person you're addressing, palm facing out.

Outdoors

clouds

Shape both hands like clouds and move them at the sides of your face.

clouds

dirty

The sign is similar to the sign for PIG except the fingers wiggle as if food is falling from one's mouth.

dirty

flower

flower

Draw your hand under your nose from one side to the other as if sniffing a flower.

grass

grass

Move your fingers toward your mouth, with your thumb out to simulate an animal eating grass. (The palm of one hand rubs underneath the chin, with your thumb out and your fingers slightly bent.)

moon

The hand is in the shape of a C and taps the side of the forehead before moving upward.

moon

rain

Your fingers are spread and fall downward at a slight angle to look like rain.

rain

sun

sun

Shape your hand like a C and look through it toward the sky. (You can also draw a circle in the sky with your index finger.)

tree

tree

Your arm is upright and supported by the back of your other hand. Your upright hand in a 5 shape pivots from the wrist to represent a tree.

wind

wind

Your hands indicate the movement of the wind by moving in a circular fashion or from side to side, with your palms facing one another.

Animals

alligator

Your hands open and close like the mouth of an alligator.

alligator

bear

Your arms cross and make a clawing motion at your chest. (Use this sign for TEDDY BEAR.)

bear

bee

Your index finger and thumb in an F shape touch your upper lip and then brush across it as if brushing away a bee.

bird

Your index finger and thumb open and close at the lips like a beak.

bug

bug

Touch your nose with the tip of your thumb. Your index and middle fingers flutter to mimic the antennae of an insect.

butterfly

butterfly

Your thumbs lock and your fingers flutter to look like a butterfly, with your palms facing toward you.

cat

From the corner of the mouth, your index finger and thumb trace a cat's whiskers.

cat

cow

Your Y-shaped hand looks like a cow horn, with the thumb touching your temple.

cow

dog

Snap your fingers together or slap your thigh.

dog

elephant

Your hand is shaped like the letter C at your nose and then slides down the body like an elephant's trunk.

elephant

fish

fish

The fingertips of one hand touch the wrist of the other hand and mimic the movement of a fish in water.

frog

frog

Your thumb, index, and middle fingers flick outward under your chin.

giraffe

giraffe

Your hand makes a grabbing motion at your neck and moves upward.

horse

horse

Two fingers wave like the ear of a horse while your thumb touches your head.

kangaroo

Your hands are held outward and jump forward to mimic a kangaroo's hopping motion.

kangaroo

lion

With your hand shaped like a claw, reach to the opposite side of your head. Then arc it back to simulate a lion's mane.

lion

monkey

monkey

Your hands scratch your sides like a monkey.

pig

pig

Your hand flaps underneath your chin, representing food dropping from a pig's mouth. (The sign is similar to DIRTY.)

rabbit

With your hands facing backward above your temples (in the opposite direction from HORSE), wiggle your index and middle fingers.

rabbit

snake

Your index and middle fingers bend to simulate snake fangs and then move forward in several small arcs.

snake

spider

spider

With your wrists crossed, link your pinkie fingers and move your hands forward while wiggling your fingers.

Bath Time

bath

Your closed hands make separate circular motions as if bathing.

bath

brush hair

Your hand simulates brushing your hair.

brush hair

brush teeth

brush teeth

Use an index finger to mimic the action of brushing your teeth.

bubbles

bubbles

Your palms are face down and your fingers flutter upward. (With an O shape in each hand, move outward one at a time, indicating bubbles in the air.)

light

Your middle finger is flicked just below your chin, with your palm facing upward.

light

mirror

Your hand is held as if it were a mirror.

mirror

shampoo

Mimic the action of washing your hair.

shampoo

soap

The fingers of one hand make a circle in the palm of the other to represent rubbing soap in the hand. (This is the same as WASH HANDS.)

soap

wash

Your closed downward hand circles your upward closed hand to simulate scrubbing.

wash

wash face

Make the sign for WASH, and then with your index finger, circle your face.

wash face

Potty Training

all done/finished

Both palms face toward you and then turn over and outward.

all done/finished

dry

The index finger wipes across the chin or upper lip as if drying it.

dry

hurry

The index and middle fingers on both hands (in an H shape) are extended and rapidly move forward in an up-and-down motion.

hurry

paper

The heel of one palm brushes against the other and toward your body.

paper

potty/toilet

potty/toilet

Your index finger folds over your bent thumb (in a T shape). With the thumb peeking out, shake your fist back and forth.

wash hands

wash hands

The fingers of one hand make a circle in the palm of the other to represent rubbing soap in the hand. (This is the same as SOAP.)

Transportation

airplane

Extend your index finger, pinkie, and thumb (like with I LOVE YOU). Move your hand out and up to simulate flight.

airplane

bicycle

Your hands mimic the action of pedaling a bike.

bicycle

boat

boat

Your hands form the shape of a boat moving through the water.

car

car

Hold your hands as if you were gripping the steering wheel of a car.

train

train

The index and middle fingers of one hand cross the same fingers on the opposite hand and move forward and backward as if the train were moving on the tracks.

truck

truck

Hold both hands as if you were gripping a large steering wheel.

Places to Go

home

The O hand shape moves from the mouth to the cheek (or from lips to temple).

outside

One hand comes out of a "hole" made by the other hand.

park

The index and middle fingers are spread and touch the upper side of the chest.

park

school

The hands clap twice to represent a teacher trying to get the attention of the class.

school

work

work

One closed fist taps the back of the other hand.

Miscellaneous

beautiful

beautiful

Your open hand circles the face as if expressing its beauty.

big

big

Bring your hands apart as if describing something large.

broken

Hold your fists together and then sharply snap them downward as if breaking a stick.

broken

medicine

The middle figure "mixes" medicine in the palm of the other hand.

medicine

present/gift

The hands mimic holding something and move forward in a gesture of giving.

present/gift

small

Bring the palms together as if indicating something small.

small

teddy bear

teddy bear

Your arms cross your chest and make a clawing motion. (This is the same as the sign for BEAR.)

Getting Everyone Involved

Everyone in your baby's life has an opportunity to help them learn sign language. Although most of these reasons have been expressed and reinforced throughout this book, what follows are ways for relatives, caregivers, and anyone else who interacts often with your child to become involved in this experience.

Why Use Baby Sign Language?

In addition to all the benefits that signing itself presents, lots of reasons exist for why everyone in the family should participate in the process:

- The baby will learn faster if more than one person is involved.

- It adds levels of interest and variety.

- Having another loving person responding to their signing efforts motivates your baby to continue.

- Your participation gives your baby an opportunity to focus on you as a separate person with a distinct presence.

- It gives the baby early insight into your unique personality.

- It establishes you as an active participant in the baby's life.

- It adds greater value to the time you spend together.

- Signing creates a stronger bond between you and the baby.

- It enables you to play an engaging and more interactive role.

- Signing establishes your role as educator and as a great playdate.

- It gives you another reason to spend time alone with the baby.

- It provides an element of structure to the time you spend together.

- It starts an early communication bond and attachment.

- It will delight the child—and you!

Tips to Help You Get Started

While you might not have as much time as you'd like with the baby, maximize the time you do have:

- Learn how to sign with and coordinate your signing plan with other family members and caregivers.

- Keep updated on the signs that have been taught as well as the baby's progress.

- Be patient. This won't happen overnight.

- Create your own signing time with the baby and make it a routine. For example, read them a book and make animal signs. Or make time to play, bond, and sign.

- Add your own personality to signing time.

- Go on walks and outings together. Talk as you go, even if the baby doesn't understand. Pay attention to what they're interested in. Sign and talk whenever you can—and appreciate the time you have.

Frequently Asked Questions About Baby Sign Language

These questions are the ones most commonly asked by parents who have started on the journey to teaching baby sign language to their child. Hopefully, the answers will help address some of your own concerns.

Will sign language interfere with my baby's speech and language development?

Research has proven conclusively that babies who sign speak earlier and have larger vocabularies than babies who don't sign. Simply put, sign language will accelerate your baby's speech and overall language development, not hinder it.

What will my baby be able to "tell" me?

Your baby can communicate when they're hungry or thirsty or they want you to read another book. They can even let you know when they have an earache or need a diaper change. It all depends on what signs you teach.

When should I begin teaching sign language to my baby?

As a general rule, around six or seven months, but it's different for each baby. To determine if your baby's ready to begin, look for signs that your baby has enough long-term memory to remember the signs and the manual dexterity to imitate them. However, because you've been speaking to your baby since birth, you can certainly begin to sign at that point too.

How fast will my baby "catch on" to signing?

Again, each baby is different. In general, if you start when your baby's around 6 or 7 months, you'll see results 8 to 10 weeks later. It depends on your baby's age and how frequent and consistent your signing efforts are. The older your baby, the faster they'll catch on. Babies who are 12 months or older might associate signs and their meanings in a matter of days rather than weeks.

When will my baby stop signing?

Most babies will stop signing once they begin to speak and are understood. But some might keep a few signs to emphasize a point or to help them when they're not being understood. Again, it all depends on the baby.

What's the most important benefit of signing with my baby?

Reduced frustration. When your baby's able to tell you what they want or need, they have little or no need to be frustrated. Life becomes less stressful for everyone.

How many signs will I have to learn?

That's up to you. This book includes more than 120 signs and they're categorized according to use. While some basic signs are recommended, after that, it's up to you and your baby.

Does this book use American Sign Language (ASL)?

Yes, the signs in this book are based on American Sign Language (ASL), the official language of the Deaf community in the United States. It's a great way to start your baby on the road to being bilingual.

Can sign language of another country be substituted?

People from other countries have said they've successfully used British Sign Language (BSL) and Irish Sign Language (ISL) with this program. It doesn't matter which sign language you use. Just follow the guidelines in this program and substitute your sign language of choice.

My baby's in daycare. How will that affect their signing?

More and more daycare centers are using sign language to communicate with the babies in their care. Among other benefits, childcare professionals have discovered less crying in a facility where babies sign. But even if your daycare provider doesn't offer signing expertise, you can still experience signing success at home. It might just take you a little longer. An even better idea? Try to convince your provider to get with the program!

My baby's more than two years old. Can they still benefit?

A baby's brain is primed for maximum language development through age 3. Plus, signing gives toddlers an outlet for expressing themselves when they can't come up with words they need. Thus, the answer is "Yes!"

Is it true that signing eliminates the "terrible twos"?

While signing might not *eliminate* the "terrible twos," it can make the stage more bearable.

Because toddlers understand more than they can express with speech at this stage, they often become frustrated. The result is a wide range of negative behaviors, including temper tantrums. Sign language gives toddlers a viable outlet to express themselves.

We speak two languages in our home. Should we sign in both?

What a wonderful opportunity for your baby! Make sure they hear and learn both languages. One parent should speak and sign in English and the other parent should speak and sign in the other language.

I've adopted a child from another country who speaks no English. Should I sign with them?

Signing won't hurt them and might even help reduce their frustration level while supporting English language learning. Just remember that your primary goal is teaching English. If you feel you can use signs as part of that, then give it a try. But if you're nervous or unsure about that, then focus on spoken English alone.

I can't seem to understand what my baby's signing. What should I do?

It depends on the situation. Try looking for additional clues. What are they looking at when they're making a certain sign? What about their body language? That might also help you decipher what they want. If you still can't figure it out, relax. It'll eventually click.

How do I motivate my baby to sign?

Try gently shaping their hands to make a certain sign or tapping them to give your baby the idea you want them to use their hands to communicate. Just remember not to use or express disappointment when it doesn't happen. Your baby will sign when they're ready.

My baby's getting their signs mixed up. How do I correct them?

You correct them with repetition and by example. It's the same way you would correct them if they said a word incorrectly. If they're making the sign for SHOES when they mean SOCKS, get out their shoes, then sign and say "SHOES." Do the same with socks. Do it a few times and they'll catch on.

My baby was making progress and now nothing's happening. What happened to their signs?

Maybe they have other things on their mind, such as teething or learning to walk or talk. Sometimes, babies just take a signing "hiatus." The important thing to remember is for you to stay on track. Keep signing as before. Chances are, they'll be back.

How do I convince my spouse and other family members this works?

Give them this book and highlight the research. But if that doesn't work, go it alone! It's too important an opportunity to pass up. My guess is that once the naysayers see how much fun you're having and how positively your baby's responding, they'll eventually join you in the effort.

What does it mean if my child uses signs without words?

It means you're doing a great job! When that happens, show your pleasure by signing back to them, but say the corresponding word a few times to encourage them to do the same. Speech takes longer to acquire, but it'll come.

Doesn't adding signing to potty training complicate the process?

Just the opposite. The signs will reinforce the routine and give nonverbal kids a way to communicate their need to use the potty.

D

Activities and Games to Encourage Your Baby to Sign

While signing should become part of your natural daily routine, activities and games that include the signs your baby already knows are an additional source of enjoyment for them. Plus, they'll serve as effective reinforcement tools.

Baby Concentration

Cut out pictures of favorite and familiar objects. Make a copy of each one. Turn them over and play Concentration. This game is an ideal way to reinforce signs when you use pictures of signing objects (BALL, BOOK, etc.). Even if your baby can't discover the "pairs," do it for them—talking and signing every step of the way as you select one object and then find its match.

Animal Cover-Up

Get out a favorite animal book and place a piece of paper over a certain animal. Then sign the animal's name. For example, ask and sign "WHERE is the LION?" Uncover the lion's picture and celebrate your "discovery," saying and signing "There's the LION!"

Hide-and-Seek

Use the sign for WHERE with objects you hide. "WHERE is the BOOK?" or "WHERE is the SHOE?" Then watch your baby's amazement as you make the object magically appear! When they're old enough, let them look for and find the object themselves.

Here's another variation: Let your baby see you hide a BALL under a blanket and let them search for it (or you find it for them). Increase their attention span and signing vocabulary by hiding two or three objects at once.

Photo Album

Nothing works better than getting out a photo album to teach signs for family members. Gently take your baby's finger and point to each member of the family while you make the sign and say the word. Make sure to point out their own picture to learn the sign BABY.

The Walking Tour

Take a walk around your house and "introduce" your baby to everyone and everything they meet. Stress the name of each object and add the sign if you know it.

The Good Night Tour

Make it a routine to sign and say good night to everyone and everything on the route to bed. After the family members, say good night to the dog, cat, even your phone. This is an opportunity to reinforce the signs.

Field Trips

A walk in the park, a trip to the zoo, an hour in the backyard—they're all educational signing adventures for your little one.

Grab Bag

Fill a laundry bag with signing objects, such as BOOK, BALL, TEDDY BEAR, etc. Then without looking, reach in the bag and pull out one of them. Make a show of it and act surprised when something comes out of the bag. Then sign and say the word.

Use Stand-Ins

While your baby's watching, "ask" their doll or teddy bear if they'd like something to EAT or DRINK. Maybe they'd prefer MILK. Maybe poor teddy bumped its head and is in PAIN. You get the idea.

Sing and Sign

Sing and sign to "Itsy Bitsy Spider," "Old MacDonald," and any other song you know. Or take a familiar melody and make up your own lyrics that include your targeted signs.

Read Books

Read as much as you can with your baby, adding signs as you go. Because babies love repetition, you can read the same book over and over.

Play Imitation Games

When your baby's very little, imitate their babbling and facial expressions. As they get older, play simple variations of Simon Says. Consider this an opportunity for expanding their babbling into related words (bah = ball).

Change Their Perspective

Give your baby an occasional new outlook on life by varying the position of their crib or moving the position of their high chair.

Use Overhead Toys and Mobiles

Make sure there's always something available to intrigue and visually interest your baby.

Make a Foggy Face

Hold your baby up to a fogged mirror. As you wipe sections clean, talk about what you see as your baby's face magically appears.

Play Peek-a-Boo

This simple activity will stimulate your baby's brain, especially when you add some surprise variations. You can reinforce several vocabulary words/signs with this game.

Problem Solving

Hide a favorite object under a blanket or pillow or in your pocket. Exaggerate your efforts until you find it. Let your baby or toddler participate in this problem-solving activity as they get older.

Play Take-Away

Place three familiar objects on the floor and talk about each one. Then put a blanket over them while "secretly" removing one. Then remove the blanket and talk about the objects that are there. See if your baby looks for the one that's missing. Keep in mind that your baby might not realize something's missing until object permanence develops at around a year old (although it can vary from 8 to 18 months). As they get older, increase the number of objects in the game.

Play Sequencing Games

Encourage your baby to imitate different clapping sequences and rhythms. Hold their hands and clap for them if they're not old enough. Or use colored blocks or colored cereal pieces as part of a sequencing activity. Say the colors out loud: "Blue, yellow, green. What comes next?" Then re-create the pattern. Make it a do-it-yourself game until your baby's old enough to participate themselves.

Smell and Touch

Let your baby smell the differences between sweet and sour. Then let them feel something silky on their hand compared with something rough, such as sandpaper or a scrub brush.

Talk to Your Baby

Speak in sentences, have conversations, ask and answer your own questions if you have to—but make sure your baby often hears the sounds and rhythms of language.

Play Music

Play classical music around the house. Or any of your favorite genres. It's a wonderful way to stimulate your baby's brain.

Play Comparisons

Line up things that are of the same category but different sizes: three shoes, three plates, etc. Then put them in size order, saying "Big, bigger, biggest." Mix them up and do it again.

Resources

These online and book sources can help you strengthen and complement what you've learned throughout this book, allowing you to enrich the baby sign language experience for your child.

Online Resources

The Internet offers a wealth of information on sign language and early childhood education. The following have been selected as great places for additional research and valuable resources to make signing with your baby easier and more enjoyable.

American Sign Language (ASL) Dictionaries

ASL Pro (www.aslpro.com): An online American Sign Language dictionary that offers more than 6,000 useful signs.

ASL Sign Language Browser (www.commtechlab.msu.edu/sites/aslweb/browser.htm): An extensive sign language dictionary of animated signs from the Communications Technology Lab at Michigan State University. This is a great complement to the dictionary in this book (Appendix A).

Continued Instruction in ASL

ASL University (www.lifeprint.com): A free resource for American Sign Language students, instructors, interpreters, and parents of Deaf children. Hearing children might also benefit.

Signing Online (www.signingonline.com): Fee-based programs that provide the basics you need to become fluent in ASL.

Baby Fingers: A Musical Journey Through Language and Learning (www.mybabyfingers.com): Live online creative sign language classes and programs for babies, children, and families.

Speech and Language Disorders

The American Speech-Language-Hearing Association (ASHA) (www.asha.org): The professional association for speech-language pathologists and audiologists. Research information on speech and language disorders and delays.

Autism Research Institute (www.autism.org): Research and resources for parents of autistic children.

Down Syndrome Resources (my.clevelandclinic.org/health/diseases/17818-down-syndrome#resources): Offers some Down syndrome organizations and websites on the topic.

Speech Delay (www.healthline.com/health/speech-delay-3-year-old-2): Information for parents and caregivers dealing with speech- and language-delayed children.

Resources for Families With Deaf Children

Hands & Voices (handsandvoices.org): This organization supports families of children who are Deaf or hard of hearing. Their approaches include ASL as well as oral communication efforts.

American Society for Deaf Children (deafchildren.org/knowledge-center/resources): Use their search engine to find local, state, and national organizations that can help you connect with other families in your local community or area.

Early Childhood Education and Development

Healthy Start (mchb.hrsa.gov/maternal-child-health-initiatives/healthy-start): Twelve booklets, each focused on one month in a baby's life. An initiative of Laura Bush when she was First Lady of Texas and now revised and distributed by the Department of Agriculture, Department of Education, and Department of Health and Human Services.

Zero to Three/Brainwonders (www.zerotothree.org/resources/529-baby-brain-map): A comprehensive and interactive resource for parents and early childhood education professionals on healthy development of children from birth to age three.

Baby Sign Language Instructor Training

Baby Sign Language Educator Course (instituteofpediatricsleep.com/baby-sign-language-educator-course): Learn how to become an instructor and teach baby sign language in your own community.

Potty Training

Baby Signs Potty Training Starter Kit: Book, DVD, motivational materials by Linda Acredolo and Susan Goodwyn. For potty training before the age of two. Search for the title and the authors' names for sellers.

Potty Train Your Child in Less Than a Day (www.drphil.com/advice/potty-train-your-child-in-less-than-a-day): From Dr. Phil, the popular host of *The Dr. Phil Show*.

Elimination Communication (www.diaperfreebaby.org): A network of free support groups promoting a natural approach to responding to elimination needs by observing a baby's signs and signals.

Books for Your Baby

Bang, Molly. *Ten, Nine, Eight.* Greenwillow, 1996.

Brown, Marc. *Play Rhymes*. Puffin, 1993.

Brown, Margaret Wise. *Goodnight Moon*. Harper Festival, 1991.

Freeman, Don. *Corduroy*. Viking Juvenile, 1968.

Glazer, Tom. *Eye Winker, Tom Tinker, Chin Chopper: 50 Musical Finger Plays*. Doubleday Books for Young Readers, 1978.

Heller, Lora. *Sign Language ABCs*. Sterling Children's Books, 2012.

Hill, Eric. *Where's Spot?* Putnam Publishing Group, 2003.

Joosse, Barbara. *Mama, Do You Love Me?* Chronicle Books, 1998.

Keats, Ezra Jack. *Peter's Chair*. Puffin Books, 1998.

Layton, Meredith. *Baby's First Words*. Peek-A-Boo Publishing, 1999.

MacMillan, Kathy. *Nita's First Signs*. Familius, 2018.

Marzollo, Jean. *I Spy Little Animals*. Cartwheel, 1998.

Miller, Margaret. *Baby Faces*. Little Simon, 1998.

—. *Peekaboo Baby*. Little Simon, 2001.

Opie, Iona (editor). *My First Mother Goose*. Candlewick, 1996.

Oxenbury, Helen. *Clap Hands*. Little Simon, 1999.

Prelutsky, Jack. *Read Aloud Rhymes for the Very Young*. Knopf Books for Young Readers, 1986.

Prochovnic, Dawn Babb. *Hip, Hip, Hooray! It's Family Day!* Magic Wagon, 2012.

Tafuri, Nancy. *Have You Seen My Duckling?* Harper Trophy, 1991.

Touch and Feel: Farm by Dorling Kindersley Publishing. DK Children, 1998.

Touch and Feel: Home by Dorling Kindersley Publishing. DK Children, 1998.

Touch and Feel: Wild Animals by Dorling Kindersley Publishing. DK Children, 1998.

Williams, Vera. *"More, More, More" Said the Baby*. Greenwillow, 1997.

Daniels, Marilyn. *Dancing With Words: Signing for Hearing Children's Literacy*. Bergin & Garvey, 2001.

Garcia, Joseph. *Sign With Your Baby: How to Communicate With Infants Before They Can Speak*. Stratton-Kehl Publications, 2000.

Pantley, Elizabeth. *The No-Cry Potty Training Solution: Gentle Ways to Help Your Child Say Good-Bye to Diapers*. McGraw-Hill, 2006.

Books for You

Acredolo, Linda, and Susan Goodwyn. *Baby Minds: Brain Building Games Your Baby Will Love*. Bantam Books, 2000.

—. *Baby Signs: How to Talk With Your Baby Before Your Baby Can Talk*. Contemporary Books, 2002.

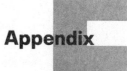

Baby Sign Language Journal

Use this journal to track your baby's signing progress: Enter the date you introduce a sign, the date your baby first attempts that sign, and the date when your baby masters that sign. Keep a copy on your refrigerator to allow babysitters or other caregivers as well as family members to communicate with your baby when you're not there.

More

Introduced: _____

First Attempt: _____

Mastered: _____

Notes: _____

_____

_____

_____

_____

_____

Eat

Introduced: _____

First Attempt: _____

Mastered: _____

Notes: _____

_____

_____

_____

_____

_____

Milk

Introduced: _____

First Attempt: _____

Mastered: _____

Notes: _____

_____

_____

_____

_____

_____

Hurt/Pain

Introduced: _____

First Attempt: _____

Mastered: _____

Notes: _____

_____

_____

_____

_____

_____

Help

Introduced: _____

First Attempt: _____

Mastered: _____

Notes: _____

_____

_____

_____

_____

_____

Diaper Change

Introduced: _____

First Attempt: _____

Mastered: _____

Notes: _____

_____

_____

_____

_____

Bottle

Introduced: _____

First Attempt: _____

Mastered: _____

Notes: _____

_____

_____

_____

_____

_____

Drink

Introduced: _____

First Attempt: _____

Mastered: _____

Notes: _____

_____

_____

_____

_____

_____

All Done/Finished

Introduced: _____

First Attempt: _____

Mastered: _____

Notes: _____

_____

_____

_____

_____

_____

Water

Introduced: _____

First Attempt: _____

Mastered: _____

Notes: _____

_____

_____

_____

_____

_____

Down

Introduced: _____

First Attempt: _____

Mastered: _____

Notes: _____

_____

_____

_____

_____

_____

Up

Introduced: _____

First Attempt: _____

Mastered: _____

Notes: _____

_____

_____

_____

_____

_____

Index

A

abstract signs, 28
activities and games, 181–184
    Animal Cover-Up, 182
    Baby Concentration, 182
    change their perspective, 183
    Comparisons, 184
    field trips, 182
    good night tour, 182
    grab bag, 182
    Hide-and-Seek, 182
    imitation games, 183
    make a foggy face, 183
    Peek-a-Boo, 183
    photo album, 182
    play music, 184
    problem solving, 183
    read books, 183
    sequencing games, 184
    sing and sign, 183
    Smell and Touch, 185
    stand-ins, 183
    Take-Away, 183
    talk to your baby, 184
    use overhead toys and
      mobiles, 183
    walking tour, 182
activities and games signs, 74–76,
  123–130. *See also* dictionary.
advanced signer, 59–96
    learning by example, 65–78
      activities and games signs,
        74–76
      animal signs, 77–78
      behavior and safety signs,
        71–74
      feelings and emotions
        signs, 76–77
      food and drink signs,
        66–69
      good manners signs, 69–71
      teaching categories, 66
    potty training, sign language
      and, 79–85
      being ready, 81

      getting an earlier start, 80
      how sign language helps
        with, 80
      readiness checklist, 81
      sequence, signs reflecting,
        81–83
      tips, 84–85
    speech skills, developing,
      87–96
      children with special needs,
        95–96
      continuing to reinforce
        signs, 88
      corrective action, taking,
        89–90
      occasions for using signs,
        89
      preference for speaking, 88
      secret signs, 90–91
      speech and language
        development concerns,
        92–95
      vocabularies used during
        transition, 89
    toddlers, sign language for,
      61–64
      benefits, 62
      information overload, 62
      plan of action, 63–64
      reasons for signing with
        toddler, 62
      talking, 64
      tips, 63
      translator, your job as, 63
AIRPLANE, 165
ALL DONE/FINISHED,
  68–69, 82, 162
    journal entry, 194
    teaching techniques, 68–69
ALLIGATOR, 146
American Sign Language
  (ASL), 4
ANGRY, 77, 110
Animal Cover-Up, 182
animal signs, 77–78, 146–156.
  See also dictionary.

APPLE, 102
ASL. *See* American Sign
  Language.

B

BABY, 137
Baby Concentration, 182
baby's first signs. *See* first signs,
  introduction of.
babysitters, enlisting help from,
  56
BALL, 75, 123
BANANA, 102
basics, 1–23
    benefits to baby (and parents),
      11–15
      baby, benefits to, 13–14
      bilingual baby, 15
      parents, benefits to, 15
      research findings, 12–13
    brain development (baby),
      17–23
      connections (synapses), 18
      experiences and, 18
      genetics and, 18
      hands, use of, 19
      IQ, boosting of, 18
      left hemisphere, 19
      sign language connection,
        18–19
      timing of, 19
      visual development, 19
      when to begin signing,
        19–21
      when to expect results,
        22–23
    description of baby sign
      language, 3–9
      appropriateness for Deaf
        babies, 7
      degree of signing success, 6
      hearing children, benefits
        to, 4–5
      IQ boost, 4

misconception, 5
native language, sign as, 7
origins of baby sign
    language, 7
receptive language skills,
    research on, 6
research projects, 7–8
as simple and natural
    communication, 4
what babies will tell you, 5–6
bath time signs, 157–161. *See also*
    dictionary.
BEAR, 146
BEAUTIFUL, 171
BED, 115
BEE, 147
beginning signs, 98–101. *See also*
    dictionary.
behavior and safety signs, 71–74,
    115–122. *See also* dictionary.
benefits to baby (and parents),
    11–15
    baby, benefits to, 13–14
        cognitive benefits, 14
        emotional benefits, 13
        language benefits, 13–14
    bilingual baby, 15
    parents, benefits to, 15
    research findings, 12–13
BICYCLE, 165
BIG, 171
big brothers and sisters, enlisting
    help from, 56
bilingual baby, 15
BIRD, 147
BOAT, 166
BOOK, 74, 85, 123
books, 183
BOTTLE, 103, 193
brain development (baby), 17–23
    connections (synapses), 18
    experiences and, 18
    genetics and, 18
    hands, use of, 19
    IQ, boosting of, 18
    left hemisphere, 19
    sign language connection, 18–19

timing of, 19
visual development, 19
when to begin signing, 19–21
    activities, 21
    jump-starting the process, 21
    making associations, 20
    manual dexterity, 20–21
    questions, 20
    sorting games, 21
when to expect results, 22–23
    perseverance, 23
    signing variables, 22–23
    timetable, 22
BREASTFEED, 103
BROKEN, 172
BROTHER, 136
BRUSH HAIR, 157
BRUSH TEETH, 158
BUBBLES, 158
BUG, 148
BUTTERFLY, 148

C

CAR, 166
CAT, 149
CLEAN, 115
clothing signs, 131–133. *See also*
    dictionary.
CLOUDS, 141
COAT, 131
cognitive benefits (baby), 14
COLD, 110
combining signs, 51
Comparisons, 184
COMPUTER, 124
COOKIE, 104
COW, 149
CRACKER, 104
CRY, 111

D

DADDY, 134
DANCE, 75, 124

description of baby sign
    language, 3–9
    appropriateness for Deaf
        babies, 7
    degree of signing success, 6
    hearing children, benefits to, 4–5
    IQ boost, 4
    misconception, 5
    native language, sign as, 7
    origins of baby sign
        language, 7
    receptive language skills,
        research on, 6
    research projects, 7–8
    as simple and natural
        communication, 4
    what babies will tell you, 5–6
DIAPER CHANGE, 83, 101
    journal entry, 192
    teaching techniques, 34–35
dictionary, 97–174. *See also* signs.
    activities and games, 123–130
        BALL, 123
        BOOK, 123
        COMPUTER, 124
        DANCE, 124
        FALL, 125
        HIDE, 125
        JUMP, 126
        MUSIC, 126
        PAINT, 127
        PLAY, 127
        RUN/CHASE, 128
        SWIM, 128
        SWING, 129
        TELEPHONE, 129
        WALK, 130
    animals, 146–156
        ALLIGATOR, 146
        BEAR, 146
        BEE, 147
        BIRD, 147
        BUG, 148
        BUTTERFLY, 148
        CAT, 149
        COW, 149

DOG, 150
ELEPHANT, 150
FISH, 151
FROG, 151
GIRAFFE, 152
HORSE, 152
KANGAROO, 153
LION, 153
MONKEY, 154
PIG, 154
RABBIT, 155
SNAKE, 155
SPIDER, 156
bath time, 157–161
BATH, 157
BRUSH HAIR, 157
BRUSH TEETH, 158
BUBBLES, 158
LIGHT, 159
MIRROR, 159
SHAMPOO, 160
SOAP, 160
WASH, 161
WASH FACE, 161
beginning signs, 98–101
DIAPER CHANGE, 101
EAT, 98
HELP #1, 100
HELP #2, 100
HURT/PAIN, 99
MILK, 99
MORE, 98
behavior and safety, 115–122
BED, 115
CLEAN, 115
DON'T TOUCH, 116
GENTLE TOUCH, 116
GOOD, 117
LISTEN, 117
NO, 118
QUIET, 118
SHARE, 119
SIT, 119
SLEEP, 120
SLOW, 120
SPEAK, 121
STOP, 121

WAIT, 122
YES, 122
clothing, 131–133
COAT, 131
HAT, 131
PANTS, 132
SHIRT, 132
SHOES, 133
SOCKS, 133
emotions and feelings, 110–114
ANGRY, 110
COLD, 110
CRY, 111
FRIGHTENED, 111
HAPPY, 112
HOT, 112
HUG, 113
I LOVE YOU, 113
LOVE, 114
SAD, 114
family, 134–137
BABY, 137
BROTHER, 136
DADDY, 134
GRANDFATHER, 135
GRANDMOTHER, 135
MOMMY, 134
SISTER, 136
feelings and emotions, 110–114
ANGRY, 110
COLD, 110
CRY, 111
FRIGHTENED, 111
HAPPY, 112
HOT, 112
HUG, 113
I LOVE YOU, 113
LOVE, 114
SAD, 114
food and drink, 102–107
APPLE, 102
BANANA, 102
BOTTLE, 103
BREASTFEED, 103
COOKIE, 104
CRACKER, 104
DRINK, 105

ICE CREAM, 105
JUICE, 106
ORANGE, 106
WATER, 107
games and activities, 123–130
BALL, 123
BOOK, 123
COMPUTER, 124
DANCE, 124
FALL, 125
HIDE, 125
JUMP, 126
MUSIC, 126
PAINT, 127
PLAY, 127
RUN/CHASE, 128
SWIM, 128
SWING, 129
TELEPHONE, 129
WALK, 130
good manners, 108–109
PLEASE, 108
SORRY, 108
THANK YOU, 109
YOU'RE WELCOME, 109
independence, 138–140
DOWN, 138
MINE, 138
UP, 139
WANT, 139
WHERE, 140
YOURS, 140
miscellaneous, 171–174
BEAUTIFUL, 171
BIG, 171
BROKEN, 172
MEDICINE, 172
PRESENT/GIFT, 173
SMALL, 173
TEDDY BEAR, 174
outdoors, 141–145
CLOUDS, 141
DIRTY, 141
FLOWER, 142
GRASS, 142
MOON, 143
RAIN, 143

SUN, 144
TREE, 144
WIND, 145
places to go, 168–170
HOME, 168
OUTSIDE, 168
PARK, 169
SCHOOL, 169
WORK, 170
potty training, 162–164
ALL DONE/FINISHED, 162
DRY, 162
HURRY, 163
PAPER, 163
POTTY/TOILET, 164
WASH HANDS, 164
safety and behavior, 115–122
BED, 115
CLEAN, 115
DON'T TOUCH, 116
GENTLE TOUCH, 116
GOOD, 117
LISTEN, 117
NO, 118
QUIET, 118
SHARE, 119
SIT, 119
SLEEP, 120
SLOW, 120
SPEAK, 121
STOP, 121
WAIT, 122
YES, 122
transportation, 165–167
AIRPLANE, 165
BICYCLE, 165
BOAT, 166
CAR, 166
TRAIN, 167
TRUCK, 167
DIRTY, 141
DOG, 150
DON'T TOUCH, 46–47, 74, 91, 116
DOWN, 138, 195
Down syndrome, 95–96

DRINK, 67, 105
journal entry, 193
teaching techniques, 67
DRY, 83, 162

E

EAT, 98
journal entry, 190
teaching techniques, 30–31, 42, 67
ELEPHANT, 150
emotional benefits (baby), 13
emotions and feelings signs, 76–77, 110–114. *See also* dictionary.
example, learning by, 65–78
activities and games signs, 74–76
BALL, 75
BOOK, 74
DANCE, 75
MUSIC, 75
RUN/CHASE, 76
animal signs, 77–78
behavior and safety signs, 71–74
DON'T TOUCH, 74
GENTLE TOUCH, 73
GOOD, 73
NO, 73
SHARE, 72
STOP, 72
feelings and emotions signs, 76–77
ANGRY, 77
HURT/PAIN, 77
food and drink signs, 66–69
ALL DONE/FINISHED, 68–69
DRINK, 67
EAT, 67
MORE, 68
good manners signs, 69–71
PLEASE, 70
SORRY, 71
THANK YOU, 70
YOU'RE WELCOME, 70–71

teaching categories, 66
express program, 37–43
activities, 39
attention-getters, 42
continuing to sign, 43
first sign, when baby makes, 41
introduction of signs, 42–43
EAT, 42
MILK, 42–43
parents-in-waiting, activities for, 43
patience, 41
perseverance, 38
significance of 11 months, 38
signing readiness, activities promoting, 43
signs still to learn, 43
steps, 38–40
homework, 39
two-week period, 39
volunteers, recruitment of, 39–40
traditional method vs. (sign introduction), 28
week 1 (introduction of first sign), 40
week 2 (staying focused and on track), 40–41
when to expect results, 38

F

FALL, 125
family, enlisting help from, 56–57
family involvement, 175–176
family signs, 134–137. *See also* dictionary.
feelings and emotions signs, 76–77, 110–114. *See also* dictionary *and* emotions and feelings signs.
field trips, 182
first signs, introduction of, 27–36
abstract signs, 28
DIAPER CHANGE, 34–35
early attempts, recognition of, 35–36

first three signs, 28–32
  EAT, 30–31
  MILK, 31–32
  MORE, 29–30
  HELP, 33–34
  HURT/PAIN, 32–33
  iconic signs, 28
  progress, signs of, 35
  recommendations, 36
  sign language categories, 28
  traditional method vs. express
    method, 28
FISH, 151
FLOWER, 142
foggy face, 183
food and drink signs, 66–69,
  102–107. *See also* dictionary.
frequently asked questions, 177–180
FRIGHTENED, 111
FROG, 151

G

games and activities. *See* activities
  and games.
games and activities signs. *See*
  activities and games signs. *See also*
  dictionary.
GENTLE TOUCH, 47, 73, 116
getting started, 25–57
  express program, 37–43
    activities, 39
    attention-getters, 42
    continuing to sign, 43
    first sign, when baby makes,
      41
    introduction of signs, 42–43
    parents-in-waiting,
      activities for, 43
    patience, 41
    perseverance, 38
    significance of 11 months, 38
    signing readiness, activities
      promoting, 43
    signs still to learn, 43
    steps, 38–40

week 1 (introduction of first
  sign), 40
week 2 (staying focused and
  on track), 40–41
when to expect results, 38
first signs, introduction of, 27–36
  abstract signs, 28
  DIAPER CHANGE, 34–35
  early attempts, recognition of,
    35–36
  EAT, 30–31
  first three signs, 28–32
  HELP, 33–34
  HURT/PAIN, 32–33
  iconic signs, 28
  MILK, 31–32
  MORE, 29–30
  progress, signs of, 35
  recommendations, 36
  sign language categories, 28
  traditional method vs. express
    method, 28
staying the course, 53–57
  getting help, 56–57
  motivational tips and tactics,
    54
  staying motivated, 54
  time constraints, 55
  tips, 57
  working outside the home,
    55–56
vocabulary, baby's sign language
  (increasing of), 45–52
  combining signs, 51
  conversation, 51–52
  DON'T TOUCH, 46–47
  GENTLE TOUCH, 47
  introducing additional signs,
    48–50
  invented signs, recording of,
    50
  sentences, signing in, 51
  setting goals, 47–48
  tips, 52
GIRAFFE, 152
GOOD, 73, 82, 117

good manners signs, 69–71,
  108–109. *See also* dictionary.
good night tour, 182
grab bag, 182
GRANDFATHER, 135
GRANDMOTHER, 135
grandparents, enlisting help from,
  56
GRASS, 142

H

HAPPY, 112
HAT, 131
hearing children, 4–5
HELP, 85, 91
  HELP #1, 100
  HELP #2, 100
  journal entry, 192
  teaching techniques, 33–34
HIDE, 125
Hide-and-Seek, 182
HOME, 168
HORSE, 152
HOT, 112
HUG, 113
HURRY, 83, 163
HURT/PAIN, 32–33, 77, 99
  journal entry, 191
  teaching techniques, 33

I

ICE CREAM, 105
iconic signs, 28
I LOVE YOU, 91, 113
imitation games, 183
independence signs, 138–140. *See
  also* dictionary.
invented signs, recording of, 50
IQ, 4, 14, 18

J

journal, 189–195
  ALL DONE/FINISHED, 194
  BOTTLE, 193
  DIAPER CHANGE, 192
  DOWN, 195
  DRINK, 193
  EAT, 190
  HELP, 192
  HURT/PAIN, 191
  MILK, 191
  MORE, 190
  UP, 195
  WATER, 194
JUICE, 106
JUMP, 126

K–L

KANGAROO, 153

language benefits (baby), 13–14
  earlier speech, 14
  early communication, 14
  larger vocabulary, 14
Late-Talker Quiz, 94
learning abilities. *See* brain
  development (baby).
learning by example, 65–78
  activities and games signs, 74–76
    BALL, 75
    BOOK, 74
    DANCE, 75
    MUSIC, 75
    RUN/CHASE, 76
  animal signs, 77–78
  behavior and safety signs, 71–74
    DON'T TOUCH, 74
    GENTLE TOUCH, 73
    GOOD, 73
    NO, 73
    SHARE, 72
    STOP, 72

feelings and emotions signs,
  76–77
    ANGRY, 77
    HURT/PAIN, 77
  food and drink signs, 66–69
    ALL DONE/FINISHED,
      68–69
    DRINK, 67
    EAT, 67
    MORE, 68
  good manners signs, 69–71
    PLEASE, 70
    SORRY, 71
    THANK YOU, 70
    YOU'RE WELCOME,
      70–71
  teaching categories, 66
LIGHT, 159
LION, 153
LISTEN, 117
LOVE, 114

M–N

manners signs, 69–71, 108–109
  PLEASE, 70, 108
  SORRY, 71, 108
  THANK YOU, 70, 109
  YOU'RE WELCOME, 70–71,
    109
manual dexterity, 20–21
MEDICINE, 172
mental acuity (baby), 3
MILK, 99
  journal entry, 191
  teaching techniques, 31–32,
    42–43
MINE, 138
MIRROR, 159
miscellaneous signs, 171–174. *See
  also* dictionary.
misconception, 5
MOMMY, 134
MONKEY, 154
MOON, 143

MORE, 29–30, 68, 98
  journal entry, 190
  teaching techniques, 29–30, 68
MUSIC, 75, 126
music, 184

native language, sign as, 7
NO, 73, 118

O

online resources, 186–187
ORANGE, 106
origins of baby sign language, 7
outdoors signs, 141–145. *See also*
  dictionary.
OUTSIDE, 168
overhead toys and mobiles, 183

P

PAINT, 127
PANTS, 132
PAPER, 82, 163
parent–infant bond, 13
PARK, 169
Peek-a-Boo, 183
photo album, 182
PIG, 154
places to go signs, 168–170. *See also*
  dictionary.
PLAY, 127
PLEASE, 70, 108
POTTY/TOILET, 164
potty training, sign language and,
  79–85
  being ready, 81
  getting an earlier start, 80
  how sign language helps with, 80
  readiness checklist, 81
  sequence, signs reflecting, 81–83
    ALL DONE/FINISHED, 82
    DIAPER CHANGE, 83
    DRY, 83

GOOD, 82
HURRY, 83
PAPER, 82
POTTY/TOILET, 81
WASH HANDS, 82
tips, 84–85
    BOOK, 85
    HELP, 85
    reward system, 85
potty training signs, 162–164. *See also* dictionary.
PRESENT/GIFT, 173
problem solving, 183

Q–R

QUIET, 118

RABBIT, 155
RAIN, 143
reading level, 14
research projects, 7–8
resources, 185–188
RUN/CHASE, 76, 128

S

SAD, 114
safety and behavior signs. *See* behavior and safety signs. *See also* dictionary.
SCHOOL, 169
secret signs, 90–91
    DON'T TOUCH, 91
    HELP, 91
    I LOVE YOU, 91
    POTTY/TOILET, 91
sentences, signing in, 51
sequencing games, 184
SHAMPOO, 160
SHARE, 72, 119
SHIRT, 132
SHOES, 133
siblings (older), enlisting help from, 56

sign
    abstract, 28
    first, 41
    iconic, 28
signing opportunities, 48–49
sign language categories, 28
signs. *See also* dictionary.
    ALL DONE/FINISHED, 68–69, 82
        journal entry, 194
        teaching techniques, 68–69
    ANGRY, 77
    BALL, 75
    BOOK, 74, 85
    BOTTLE, 103
        journal entry, 193
    DANCE, 75
    DIAPER CHANGE, 34–35, 83
        journal entry, 192
        teaching techniques, 34–35
    DON'T TOUCH, 74, 91
        teaching techniques, 46–47
    DOWN, 138
        journal entry, 195
    DRINK, 67
        journal entry, 193
        teaching techniques, 67
    DRY, 83
    EAT, 30–31, 42
        journal entry, 190
        teaching techniques, 30–31, 42, 67
    GENTLE TOUCH, 47, 73
    GOOD, 73, 82
    HELP, 85, 91
        journal entry, 192
        teaching techniques, 33–34
    HURRY, 83
    HURT/PAIN, 32–33, 77
        journal entry, 191
        teaching techniques, 33
    I LOVE YOU, 91
    MILK, 31–32, 42–43
        journal entry, 191
        teaching techniques, 31–32, 42–43

MORE, 68
    journal entry, 190
    teaching techniques, 29–30
MUSIC, 75
NO, 73
PAPER, 82
PLEASE, 70
POTTY/TOILET, 81, 91
RUN/CHASE, 76
SHARE, 72
SORRY, 71
STOP, 72
TELEPHONE, 28
THANK YOU, 70
UP, journal entry, 195
WASH HANDS, 82
WATER, journal entry, 194
YOU'RE WELCOME, 70–71
sing and sign, 183
SISTER, 136
SIT, 119
SLEEP, 120
SLOW, 120
SLP. *See* speech and language pathologist.
SMALL, 173
Smell and Touch, 184
SNAKE, 155
SOAP, 160
SOCKS, 133
SORRY, 71, 108
sorting games, 21
SPEAK, 121
special needs, children with, 95–96
speech and language pathologist (SLP), 95
speech skills, developing, 87–96
    children with special needs, 95–96
    continuing to reinforce signs, 88
    corrective action, taking, 89–90
    occasions for using signs, 89
    preference for speaking, 88
    secret signs, 90–91
        DON'T TOUCH, 91
        HELP, 91

I LOVE YOU, 91
POTTY/TOILET, 91
speech and language
 development concerns, 92–95
  definitions, 92
  development timeline, 93–94
  Late-Talker Quiz, 94
  syntax, 92
  taking action, 95
 vocabularies used during
  transition, 89
SPIDER, 156
stand-ins, 183
staying the course, 53–57
 getting help, 56–57
 motivational tips and tactics, 54
 staying motivated, 54
 time constraints, 55
 tips, 57
 working outside the home, 55–56
STOP, 72, 121
SUN, 144
SWIM, 128
SWING, 129
syntax, 92

T

Take-Away, 183
teaching techniques
 activities and games signs, 74
 ALL DONE/FINISHED, 68–69
 animal signs, 77–78
 behavior and safety signs, 72
 DIAPER CHANGE, 34–35
 DON'T TOUCH, 46–47
 DRINK, 67
 EAT, 30–31, 42, 67
 feelings and emotions signs,
  76–77
 food and drink signs, 66
 GENTLE TOUCH, 47
 good manners signs, 70
 HELP, 33–34
 HURT/PAIN, 33
 MILK, 31–32, 42–43

MORE, 29–30, 68
 potty training, 84
TEDDY BEAR, 174
TELEPHONE, 28, 129
THANK YOU, 70, 109
toddlers, sign language for, 61–64
 benefits, 62
 information overload, 62
 plan of action, 63–64
 reasons for signing with toddler,
  62
 talking, 64
 tips, 63
 translator, your job as, 63
traditional method, express method
 vs. (sign introduction), 28
TRAIN, 167
transportation signs, 165–167. *See
 also* dictionary.
TREE, 144
TRUCK, 167

U–V

UP, 139, 195

visual development, 19
vocabulary, baby's sign language
 (increasing of), 45–52
 combining signs, 51
 conversation, 51–52
 DON'T TOUCH, 46–47
 GENTLE TOUCH, 47
 introducing additional signs,
  48–50
  baby's lead, following of, 49
  baby's own inventions, 50
  being prepared, 49–50
  creating signing
   opportunities, 49
  identifying signing
   opportunities, 48–49
 invented signs, recording of, 50
 sentences, signing in, 51
 setting goals, 47–48
 tips, 52

W

WAIT, 122
WALK, 130
walking tour, 182
WANT, 139
WASH, 161
WASH FACE, 161
WASH HANDS, 82, 164
WATER, 107, 194
WHERE, 140
WIND, 145
WORK, 170

X–Y–Z

YES, 122
YOU'RE WELCOME, 70–71, 109
YOURS, 140